IDLE HOUR ROMP

Boyhood Adventures in

Mid-20th Century Oakdale

By

Stephen C. Carlisle

Third Edition

ISBN: 148270840X
ISBN-13: 9781482708400

The "Idle Hour" Series

Idle Hour Romp - Boyhood Adventures in Mid-20th Century Oakdale

Idle Hour Gardens - Growing Up in Mid-20th Century Oakdale

Idle Hour Tribe - Family, Friends and Neighbors in Mid-20th Century Oakdale

Wild Blue Yonder - Beyond Idle Hour and Mid-20th Century Oakdale

Idle Hour Retrospect - A Native Son's Study of 20th Century Oakdale

To Butch

Contents

FOREWORD

"Everybody needs his memories. They keep the wolf of insignificance from the door."

--- Saul Bellow

In spurts my mind was wont to reminisce. Occasionally and unpredictably, I was inspired to write about particular memories, seeking to capture each one in words, giving it substance so that it could exist outside of my mind and be saved forever, making it (and therefore me) immortal. I did this mostly for my own pleasure but shared my writings with my family as they came. The family enjoyed them and encouraged me to continue.

At first I wrote the memoirs randomly, as the muse called, with no plan or sense of order. Over time they accumulated and wanted to be organized and eventually, professionally printed. And so, this book. Or I should say books because this is the first of several.

I describe my experiences as I remember them, set in the context of their happening, never questioning my memory. Sometimes when I compare my recollections to those of friends who shared the same experiences, I find that our accounts differ. I am amazed. How could my friends get it wrong? I have come to realize that memory, even my own, is not infallible.

It doesn't matter. Memories are what they are and in my mind they are reality. I think of them as little time capsules, set in the context of their happening. I play them back in their own periods, unembellished by later events or other accounts.

It is tempting to go back and revise the memoirs based on things I learned in later years, but I resist. In a few instances I add notes referring to things I learned later, but only to confirm or reinforce the original episode without changing it. And in some cases I attach latter day photos but again only as a footnote to reflect on the memory without intruding. For now, I present my boyhood as I remember it. Correction can come later.

PART 1 - BEGINNINGS

Like pearls on a string

And leaves floating on a pond

Memories suspended

Leaves on a Pond

Scattered through the attic of my mind lie a number of early disjointed snapshot memories. They are the earliest, including what must be the first. Each one stands alone, without continuity or frame of reference. They may or may not be real. With hindsight, a time-line of sorts can be reconstructed but there is no organization in memory. They float, like leaves on a pond.

* * * * * * * * * * * * *

Brown shoes. Brown pants from the knee down to wide cuffs above the shoes. A brown satchel nearby. The picture is stark, partial. Nothing above the man's knees. Little texture, little color. No sound. I don't see me but I am very small, sitting on the bare floor in the foyer of the house on Woodlawn Avenue. It is the day my father left.

Another frame, same place and posture but no visual save the empty foyer. "Stevie get your shoes on, we're going to take Daddy's car to the garage." My sister's voice, probably Nancy's.

(Years later, I was in the Air Force, home on leave, sitting at the bar in Burke's Log Cabin with old Tom O'Neill, a local character who ran the garage on the corner of Idle Hour Boulevard and Montauk Highway. I recounted the story because I remembered it was Tom's garage that we took the car to. To my amazement, Tom said he remembered the car and the incident. He had bought the car, told me what he paid for it but I don't remember the amount.)

* * * * * * * * * * * * *

Red snow suit.   Woolen and fuzzy, with a hat or hood and mittens to match.   Bundled against the cold, Granddaddy carried me on his shoulders the block and a half to the West Gate House where he lived with Grandmama and Aunt Edith.   There he made me the best oatmeal in the world.   His special way of slow cooking it made it extra creamy.

* * * * * * * * * * * * * *

Swans.   Huge magnificent white birds with long graceful necks and orange beaks.   The house at the foot of Woodlawn was across Connetquot Boulevard from the Connetquot River.   The swans, always a pair and sometimes with a brood of young, would swim in the river and come ashore near the house on Woodlawn.   If you got too near the adult male would advance and threaten with a fearsome hissing sound.   You retreated.

The river at Woodlawn …

* * * * * * * * * * * * * *

A long, narrow footbridge at the foot of Woodlawn connected an island (later known as Ongania's island) in the Connetquot upon which stood a large stucco home.   Two lovely old sisters named Burke lived in the house on the island.   They were from the Bahamas and had a colored servant named Pauline.

* * * * * * * * * * * * * *

A huge tree from our yard, oak I think, was felled by a hurricane straight across Woodlawn Avenue so that the school bus couldn't pass.   There was no school for my sisters that day.   (1)

Tree across
Woodlawn …
9/15/44

* * * * * * * * * * * * * *

We had moved to the house on Roxbury but Grandmama, Granddaddy and Aunt Edith still lived in the West Gate House. Nancy, Mary and I were returning from a visit, I being conveyed in a baby carriage, apparently too young to walk such a distance. Near dusk, we approached the Clock Tower coming down Idle Hour Boulevard when one of the girls flipped the hood-type cover on the carriage from front to back so that I could see what they saw: Beyond the arches, in front of Alice Johnson's residence, figures in flowing gossamer clothes appeared to be dancing, ballet-style, in the street. The girls pushed the baby carriage very fast, took the corner in front of the Clock Tower on two wheels, ran through Hetzel's driveway and we were home in a minute, wide-eyed and breathless.

Where they danced …

* * * * * * * * * * * * * *

The yard in back of the house on Roxbury was not very big but it seemed so to me when I was very small. It was large enough to hold a small house trailer, where Doris Marcell lived for a time. I remember Mama standing on the step to the door of that small trailer, crying … President Roosevelt had died. I knew little of the man but he must have been important because his death caused my mother to cry. I think Doris cried too. (2)

* * * * * * * * * * * * * *

Upstairs in the house on Roxbury, middle of the night, awakened from deep sleep. From the small window I could see orange flames leaping into the night from the line of buildings adjoining the Clock Tower. A spectacular fire, it destroyed the roofs and interiors of much of the Artist Colony's brick buildings. Alice Johnson's residence was damaged. A mess. She paid us kids ten cents a bucket to haul debris down from her upstairs. (3)

* * * * * * * * * * * * * *

Mama gave me two pot covers to bang together, to make noise in celebration. We (local citizens, I don't remember how many) paraded down Idle Hour Boulevard leading to the Clock Tower. Claude Gonvierre, the music teacher and friend to my mother who lived in the Clock Tower invited us in. We climbed several flights of stairs to the level where the big bell over the arch was. The bell was outside the brick wall but attached inside to a large L-shaped iron handle. We rocked the big handle back and forth and the heavy bell tolled loudly. It was VJ day. (4)

The bell is about half way up, in the ivy to the right of the clock ...

* * * * * * * * * * * * *

School age begins a whole new era for my collection of memories. The structure of successive grades, cradled and ordered in time, gives continuity to the events that become memory so from kindergarten on, most, but not all, of my memories are connected, one to another, more like pearls on a string than leaves on a pond.

18

Notes

Long after I wrote "Leaves On A Pond", research led me to the archives of the "Suffolk County News", a local Long Island newspaper based in Sayville but covering the surrounding communities as well. A Long Island institution, the paper has been published weekly without interruption since 1884. To my delight, I found some items relevant to my very vague "floating" memories:

(1) **9/15/1944** *A hurricane that swept up the New Jersey and Long Island coast Sept. 14 raged here from seven o'clock to midnight, reaching a peak of 90 miles an hour, uprooting trees and breaking plate glass windows, but fortunately doing no great damage to Fire Island Beach, where the dunes have been left practically intact. There was no loss of life in this area and no casualties.*

9/22/1944 *Shortly after the hurricane subsided last week, highway Department Foreman William Stochl Jr. rounded up and routed out his gang of men and they went on their way to clear the roads of fallen trees and branches. In the Oakdale Idle Hour section of the Bohemia Highway Division, trees with a girth of two feet or more were chopped away and disposed of in short order.*

(2) **4/13/1945** *President Franklin Delano Roosevelt died almost without warning of a cerebral hemorrhage at 4:35 p.m. on April 12 at Warm Springs, Georgia. Harry Truman became president that same day at 7:09 p.m.*

(3) **5/04/1945** *A disastrous fire that destroyed three homes and resulted in damage to a fourth, swept the Tower Mews of the Artist Colony in Oakdale, destroying the famous Vanderbilt clock tower and many valuable antiques and, at times, threatening the entire colony despite the heroic efforts of the West Sayville firemen. The fire is believed to have been caused by a spark flying from a fireplace in the neighborhood.*

6/01/1945   *Claude Gonvierre of Oakdale is busy with plans for the rebuilding of his home recently destroyed by fire.*

(4)   **8/10/1945**   *As "The Suffolk County News" went to press on Aug. 10 the world was awaiting an announcement by President Truman to confirm or deny the jubilant rumor that Japan was about to surrender and that peace and victory at long last would be ours. Everyone was waiting for the official announcement from the White House.*

8/17/1945   *At four minutes past seven o'clock on Tuesday evening, Aug. 14, the Sayville fire siren began to wail—if the sustained and raucous scream that has sounded for many an air raid drill since the attack on Pearl Harbor, could be called a wail, proclaiming as it did: There is peace, there is victory!   From out of the homes along Candee Avenue and Collins and Lincoln, the women and the middle-aged men and the boys, started to shout to their neighbors over fences.   There were few in the crowd for whom the end of the war did not hold special promise.*

The House on Woodlawn

At the foot of Woodlawn Avenue where it meets the river, there was a big stucco house, one of just a handful scattered along Woodlawn in 1942 when my family moved to Idle Hour from Minnesota. I was a mere seven months old that April when we moved into the house on Woodlawn.

The house was built in the Spanish style, complete with porticos and white stucco exterior and curved orange roof tiles. The site where it stood was a particularly good one, on the Connetquot River at its beginnings where it starts to widen from stream to river, just a stone's throw upriver from the big Vanderbilt mansion. Directly across Connetquot Drive was a large home on an island in the river that could only be reached by a narrow foot bridge.

We lived in the house on Woodlawn for about two and a half years, moving to a smaller house on Roxbury Avenue sometime in late '44 or early '45. My memories from the time I lived in the big Spanish house are naturally few and vague but the house holds a special place in my heart.   Although we no longer lived there, it was not far from the little house on Roxbury, well within my Idle Hour stomping grounds, and was a familiar part of my boyhood landscape.

1943

2009

Eden

Awakening was gradual. From a tiny center, my universe grew in a slow motion burst of awareness, a "Little Bang" of expanding consciousness, moving slowly at first, ever more quickly as I and my world grew. For the first decade my world was limited, thankfully, to things I could easily absorb. This was good. By whatever Providence, I was not burdened with the overwhelming knowledge that came in later years. Life was simple.

The time of my youth was that era of optimism and growth and innocence in America that followed the national traumas of the Great Depression and World War II. Of course I knew very little of these things at the time but they were deeply embedded in the society around me. It was a good time to be young and growing up.

The center of my expanding universe was a small house on Roxbury Avenue. A modest house, stucco and wood on the outside, one and a half stories, one bathroom, coal-fired furnace in a dingy basement. Living room, dining room, kitchen and small bathroom on the main floor. Sparsely furnished. A narrow, winding staircase led to an open area used as a bedroom by my mother, and two small bedrooms tucked beneath the eaves of the sloping roof. The space upstairs was cramped but livable. The little house on Roxbury was my home, my haven, for eleven of my most formative years.

The yard surrounding the house, perfectly natural with gentle slopes and gullies, rolling from cultivated front to wild rear, was my own personal playground. A rickety wooden lattice fence, with an arbor opening in the center, traversed the back yard. Back in one corner, past the fence, was a playhouse. About 12' x 12', it had a door, three windows and a small 5' x 5' extension on one side. The low, flat roof made a wonderful fort-like perch from which I repelled countless imaginary attackers.

To me the yard seemed larger than it really was. It was a botanical wonder. Concord grape vines, strung with big, juicy purple grapes, climbed the arbor and part of the fence. Inside the fence a variety of fruit trees grew, scattered here and there: two very large wild cherry, two apple, one each of pear, peach and mulberry. Blackberries and raspberries grew inside the fence on one side; wild strawberries grew in a large open field outside the fence. In the woods beyond the field were blueberry and huckleberry bushes and more wild cherry trees. All this fruit was edible, some more so than others.

In the spring we'd plant a vegetable garden in the field out back: radishes, carrots, string beans, onions, lettuce … we'd plant the seeds that came in little paper packets and then put the empty packets on sticks to mark the garden rows. Wild mint and scallions grew on one side of the house. All of these we savored.

Several large trees … oak, hickory, silver maple … were scattered around the yard. These were great for climbing. There was a small multi-trunked white birch out front of the house. On one side of the front door was a large spruce tree, on the other a flowering dogwood. There was another dogwood in the back yard. Also in back, on the southeast edge was a row of three or four cedars.

And there were flowers and flowering bushes: purple and white lilacs, forsythia and climbing roses; daffodils, iris, violets and lilies of the valley; periwinkle, dandelions, and clover; and some others whose names I didn't know.

Near the northwestern border of the yard, toward the back, was a little cement pond shaped like a shamrock. It was very small but a nice home, off and on, to a frog or two and some goldfish. Not far from the pond was a small mound of rocks and weeds and flowers that my mother called a rock garden, the creative, neglected work of some previous resident.

Life was simple in those early years. The little stucco house and the yard full of natural treasures were sublimely compatible with the wonder and innocence of childhood. Here was my playground, filled with stimulating things that became familiar and comfortable. Here was my sanctuary, insulated from the unknown and the fearsome. Here I thrived … here I learned … Here was my Garden of Eden.

Inevitably, I had to leave.

Stevie, Nancy & Gene on the fence out back ...

Mary, Wiggles, Nancy & Chessie in the back yard ...

Stevie at the north corner ...

Happy at the front step ...

Heaven's view of my Garden of Eden ...

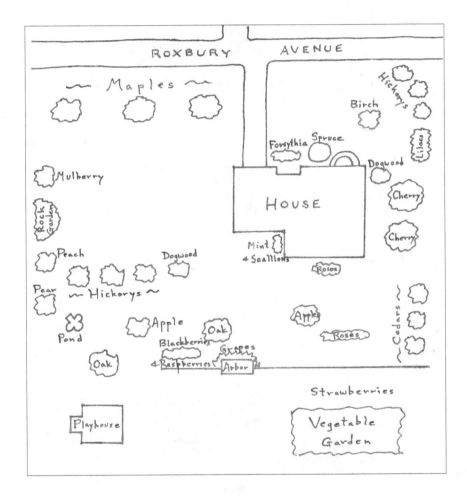

Innocence prevails

In the Garden of Eden

Both are left behind

Seasons

Seasons came and went at the little house on Roxbury, in a comfortable, natural rhythm. I was growing, but didn't realize it. Things changed, but stayed the same.

Winters in the little house could be hard. The coal-fired furnace in the basement was tricky to manage, and if the fire went out during the night, which it frequently did, in the morning you could see your breath when you stuck your head out from under the covers. It was very hard leaving the warmth of your cocoon. When you finally did, getting dressed for school was an adventure.

But winter always brought Christmas, and Christmas was a happy time. We'd paint Christmassy things on the inside of the windows with poster paints, things that didn't take much artistic ability, wreaths and holly and candles and snowmen. We always had a real Christmas tree, strung with those old-fashioned lights that all went out when one went out. We put the tinsel on the tree one strand at a time. Sleep on Christmas Eve was impossible. Gifts on Christmas morning were few and modest, all the more appreciated.

Eventually spring would come, heralded by the Pussy Willows, followed in quick order by the forsythia and daffodils and finally the lilacs. It was time to take down the storm windows, which we'd put up the previous Fall, and put up the screens in their place. It was a semi-annual ritual, swap whatever was hanging in the windows with whatever was stacked in the garage. Easter came early in spring and we always got a new outfit to wear. The weather became perfect. Cool May days got warmer as everything grew in a green and pastel explosion of life.

Then summer came and we'd burst with the freedom of it … "No more pencils, no more books, no more teachers' dirty looks…" The endless, carefree summer before us, I'd shed shoes and shirt and not put them back on until September. "Bare footie" and shirtless, I roamed and played from dawn 'til dusk every day through the endless summer. We went swimming in the river and the bay and in Second Pond. At night in the yard we'd catch as many of the ubiquitous fireflies as we could and put them in a mayonnaise jar with holes in the top, punched with an ice pick. We struggled to sleep in the sweltering summer nights, grateful for the relief of an occasional breeze.

But, alas, the endless summer was not endless. August would run out and a new school year would start right after Labor Day, within a few days of my birthday, a bitter-sweet coincidence. September weather was always perfect, challenged only by the May weather which was perfect in a different way. Warm September days got cooler as the trees flamed out in a blaze of glory.

October brought chill mornings and the exhilaration of seeing your breath at the bus stop. The brisk air and autumn color of the leaves told you that Halloween was nigh … that wonderful night of madness when you got to pretend to be what you were not and act outrageous and collect goodies from the neighbors.

Thanksgiving would come, a pleasant comforting interval. We'd gather at Grandmama's little log cabin, the tiny living room completely filled by Aunt Edith's table, wings opened, for the grownups, and a card table for the kids. The feast was special and always included apple and pumpkin and mince pies. We found security in the tradition of it all.

And then again it was winter, which could be hard in the little house on Roxbury.

The "Big Snow" Christmas 1947 ...

(Courtesy Donald A. Rogers)

IDLE HOUR ROMP

Donnie, Paulie   Stevie, Carol Lynn, Moira

Easter ... Stevie & Nancy

Stevie & Butch - July 1950

The Roxbury House - July 1995

Moo Cow

The little kid was standing at the end of the dirt trail that meandered through the yard behind the big rundown abandoned Tudor house on the corner of Roxbury and Oceanview. This old house was a familiar but inert part of the landscape. Obviously grand at one time, it was cold and lifeless now, windows broken, yard neglected. But on this day, there were humans present, and the one I remember vividly was a little towheaded kid, about my age, maybe four years old.

He stood straight and stiff at the end of the drive, near the edge of Roxbury Avenue, facing me as I, looking askance, strolled by. "We're gonna get a moo cow" he declared, with serious conviction and enthusiasm.

I knew nothing about this kid, or his circumstances, or of life anywhere beyond my tiny little world on Roxbury Avenue, but I sensed intuitively that here was a "city" kid, whatever that was, whose family was looking for a place in the country, and maybe this abandoned old Tudor with its big yard was it, and this kid was excited by tales told by his parents of life in the country. Tales like getting a "moo cow".

I could imagine his father telling him, " … and we'll get some chickens, and ducks ….. and a moo cow … and live off the fat of the land." And the kid, in his innocence, wanted to share his anticipation with everyone he met in this new, country environment. That included me, walking by, inspecting this strange little naïve city kid with more than a little skepticism. "Moo cow"? "Moo cow"?? Jeez.

Well it came to pass, after a time, several months maybe, that a family moved into the big old Tudor, fixing the windows and making the place livable again. The family included a kid my age but he wasn't the towheaded, "moo cow" kid. He was Butch Hetzel, who was to become my brother and best friend.

The little towheaded kid at the end of the drive was Butch's cousin, Jody Von Der Vor, who became another brother and best friend and eventually, brother-in-law. He and his family moved into a big Mediterranean house on the Grand Canal, about half a mile from Roxbury Avenue.

Butch and Jody and I grew up together in that rural heaven. We ran the fields and woods and waterways with abandon. We played football and baseball on the lawn around the huge old Vanderbilt mansion. We swam and rafted and boated and fished in the river and ponds and canals in summer and skated on them in winter. We built huts and forts and treehouses wherever we could. We camped out often in the woods that were more prevalent than houses and yards.

We caught trout in the headwaters of the Connetquot, sunfish in Second Pond, snappers in the river, blowfish in the bay and crabs in the canals. We took clams out of the bay by "treading" them with our bare feet. We'd take great big snapping turtles out of the canals and chop off their heads because they were as nasty as they were ugly and they ate the baby ducks. We hunted rabbit and squirrel and pheasant and quail and chippie birds in the untamed fields and woods.

We enjoyed a care-free, fun-filled, happy, country childhood in the Oakdale of the '40s and '50s. Hetzels had a horse named Whitey and a duck named Yogi. Jody had a raccoon named Rocky. Everyone had dogs and cats. But no one ever got a "moo cow".

The Tudor house from Roxbury …

The tow headed kid …

(Courtesy Joseph Von Der Vor)

The Sosnilo/Von Der Vor Mediterranean …

(Courtesy Joseph Von Der Vor)

PART 2 - SCENES

The rooms of the romp

River and field and castle

Boyhood's friendly womb

The Connetquot

The Connetquot River is a crescent-shaped body of water in the middle of the south shore of Long Island. Not much of a river by continental standards it is a significant natural feature on Long Island. From an Indian name meaning "great river", Connetquot is pronounced con-NET-quot by most, CON-na-qut or CON-na-QUOT by some. I prefer the former.

The river flows south in the beginning, curving gradually to the east and after three miles or so merges with the Great South Bay. Only a few yards wide at its source, it opens to nearly a mile at its mouth, looking from above like a great cornucopia.

The headwaters are fresh, coming from several feeder lakes and streams, but as you move downriver the water becomes increasingly brackish. Eventually river becomes bay which of course is a branch of the Atlantic Ocean.

The headwaters looking down river …

At the mouth looking east toward Great South Bay …

Late in the 19th century, the wild, pristine area around the Connetquot drew the attention of New York's millionaire tycoons, and the river became sandwiched between large estates of two of the richest. William Bayard Cutting's thousand acre "Westbrook" was on the west bank, and William Kissam Vanderbilt's nine hundred acre "Idle Hour" was on the east bank.

At the heart of Idle Hour, Vanderbilt's huge brick and sandstone mansion overlooks the Connetquot at the river's beginnings:

Cutting's mansion was grand, too, but not so grand or near to the river as Vanderbilt's.   From mid-river it appears small:

As the age of the tycoons passed, more plebian settlements grew up in and around the estates, Great River on the west bank, Oakdale on the east. On the Great River side in addition to the Bayard Cutting Arboretum in the north there was the Timber Point Country Club in the south and a number of private homes in between. The Oakdale side was mostly Idle Hour with some marshland in the southeast that had once been part of Pepperidge Hall, another tycoon's estate that was in ruins by 1940.

Lodged in the mouth of the river, between Timber Point and Pepperidge Hall, was a flat, treeless, marshy island that we called "the point", a description of the sand spit on the north side that jutted out towards the mainland and served as divider between river and bay. On the west side of the island was "the cut", a narrow waterway separating the island from the Timber Point golf course and connecting the Connequot to the Great South Bay. The island itself probably had a formal name but we always referred to it as just "the point".

Idle Hour was distinguished by many remnants of the Vanderbilt estate. Directly on the river there was the mansion at the headwaters and the quaint little wooden, brick and stucco Tea House at the mouth. Between the mansion and the Tea House there were connecting canals, inroads from the river into the interior of the estate dug by gangs of laborers at the turn of the century.

The Grand Canal ...

In the post-estate era most of the upper river Idle Hour shore became residential, save of course the mansion itself, but the lower half mile or so was commercial.   In quick succession there was Zaccone's Boatyard, Snapper Inn, Muff's Boatyard, Hotel Pirnat (the Tea House), the Idle Hour Taxpayer's Association Clubhouse and Snug Harbor.   Each of these had a distinct character of its own.

The idyllic Connetquot River with its park-like estate surroundings made one huge playground for the lucky kids who lived in Great River and Oakdale.   We swam and rafted and boated and fished in it whenever it wasn't frozen over and skated on it when it was.   It was a carefree kid's paradise in the 1950's.

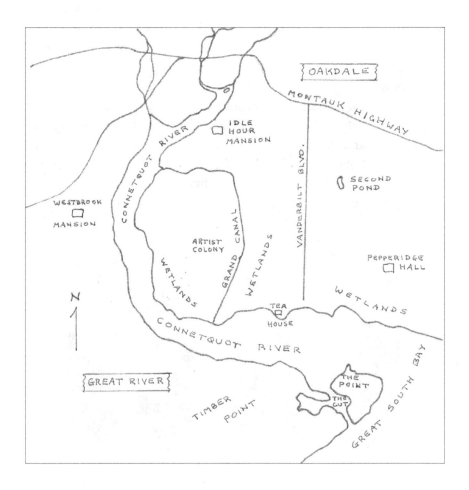

Ide Lour

Vanderbilt's double-entendre was lost on me. I always thought of Idle Hour as simply a geographical area, not as a period of inactivity or a time of leisure. We pronounced it "Ide Lour" and it was our neighborhood, essentially that part of Oakdale bounded by the Connetquot River, Montauk Highway and Vanderbilt Boulevard. Many years later I came to appreciate the millionaire's cleverness in naming his lavish retreat but the thought never formed in my young mind.

Ide Lour was home to me ... still is, albeit in memory only. The old neighborhood is still there, recognizable but changed beyond sentimental reverie. Today it is crowded, over-built, manicured ... sculpted more by the hand of man than of God. Progress, I suppose.

I knew very little of the super-rich man and the estate that he named Idle Hour. There were bits of obscure local mythology, interesting but unimportant. What I cared about were the woods and fields and waterways and ruined old buildings that my friends and I could play in and on and around.

The area was quaintly disorganized ... the roads primitive, most paved, a few not, some straight, others winding and irregular ... the whole a pleasant mixture of careful planning and random accident. Overall there were more natural spaces than human constructions. Even the canals and lagoons that we knew to be man-made seemed like natural waterways, fitting into the wilder character of Ide Lour and connecting seamlessly to the Connetquot River. The canals and adjacent marshlands were home to many native aquatic and swamp creatures ... all kinds of fish, reptiles, birds; some mammals.

There were buildings scattered throughout the largely undeveloped area, in some cases clustered, in others isolated. The architecture of these buildings was eclectic, a word I would not have used back then but one that describes perfectly the mixture of styles, a mixture strongly suggestive of different historical eras.

Most obvious were the Vanderbilt buildings, characterized by their brick and stone construction or Tudor-style stucco and timber. The huge mansion and the Artist Colony were predominate. The mansion, and the adjoining Coach House, were occupied by the National Dairy company throughout my boyhood years. The original Vanderbilt Farm became the Artist Colony after the Vanderbilts left. With its imposing Clock Tower and converted brick farm buildings, the area had a distinct character all its own. I grew up a block away from the Artist Colony, virtually in the shadow of the Clock Tower.

Some of the other Vanderbilt buildings were known to us for what they were and they had descriptive names: the Tea House, the Power House, the Ice House, the East & West Gate Houses. Others blended into the eclectic mixture as part of the landscape but we were unaware of their Vanderbilt significance, they were just somebody's home: Bjorkman's, Trautwein's, Carlson's Inn, Thompson's, Hetzel's, Frank Martin's.

After the Vanderbilt buildings came the Spanish and Mediterranean types, looking old and historical but easily recognized as post-Vanderbilt. They were reminiscent of silent movie era Hollywood or the Great Gatsby's Roaring Twenties. Notable among these were the House on Woodlawn, the Sosnilo's Mediterranean and the Skey's Italian Provincial on Beverly Road.

There were a fair number of smaller houses and bungalows, scattered throughout Idle Hour but especially concentrated in the area below the Artist Colony. These suggested summer residence and very often that's just what they were. Many families lived in the city most of the year and spent the summer out on the Island.

To round out the great variety of architectural styles there were an increasing number of more modern, wood frame houses, typical of post-war suburbia. Many of these were added, one at a time, as I grew up.

There was none of the sameness in Idle Hour that you find in cities and modern suburbs, no cookie-cutter development … each building was unique … each person was unique … yet they all, buildings and people, fit into one harmonious whole, a place we called Ide Lour.

The Artist Colony

Very near to Roxbury Avenue was the Artist Colony, an unusual little neighborhood, strangely different from any other. In fact, it was unique.

Two blocks east of Roxbury, it was a square area about five hundred feet on a side. The sides of the square were four streets: Tower Mews, Featherbed Lane, Jade Street and Hollywood Drive. The square was trisected within by two narrow, parallel lanes, one called Princess Gate, the other just a dirt trail with no name. The street names were quaint, reminiscent of Victorian England, but that didn't matter to me back in 1950 when I was eight years old.

The defining landmark and anchor of the Artist Colony was the Clock Tower, standing at the corner of Tower Mews and Hollywood Drive. Square based, nine stories high, made of red brick, the Clock Tower dominated the area. Halfway up the north side of the tower was a huge iron clock face that gave the structure its name. On the west side, also halfway up was a large iron bell that could be rung by hand from inside the tower.

The Clock Tower guarded the western entrance to the Artist Colony. This entrance was framed by a pair of brick arches that spanned Tower Mews and connected the Clock Tower to a smaller, more conventional red brick building. This smaller building, someone's residence, was in turn connected by a high brick wall that ran southward down Tower Mews and attached to Alice Johnson's two-story, red brick abode. This wall had several large window-like openings with massive granite sills about seven feet off the ground. The area behind the wall was in ruin, filled with debris from the catastrophic fire I witnessed in 1945.

Princess Gate was a narrow dirt and gravel trail, barely wide enough for a car, running at right angles from Tower Mews through to Jade Street. On either side of Princess Gate were some long, low brick buildings, so low that the floors were a foot or two below ground level. Local lore had it that the original purpose of these buildings was to house the various and numerous animals of the long ago Vanderbilt Farm. These long buildings were divided into many different sections ... stables, pig pens, chicken coops and the like, I supposed. In my era, some of these sections were deserted and in ruin but others had been fashioned into apartments where people lived.

Featherbed Lane, wider and better paved than Princess Gate ran parallel to it, also connecting Tower Mews and Jade. At the corner of Tower Mews and Featherbed was a large man-made pond we called the Fish Pond. Elliptical, about 60 x 90 feet, it had concrete outer walls and a small island, also with concrete walls, in the center. The water was a foot or two deep.

In summer the Fish Pond was filled with lily pads and goldfish and frogs. The frogs produced little black, rubbery babies, tadpoles, that we called pollywogs. We delighted in scooping out the little pollywogs and putting them in jars, like we did with fireflies on summer nights, just to see how many we could catch. We'd let them go when we tired of the game. In winter the Fish Pond froze solid very easily, much sooner than the canals or the river. I learned to skate at an early age on this friendly and convenient little rink, using my sisters' hand-me-down white figure skates.

Featherbed Lane ran eastward from the Fish Pond at Tower Mews about five hundred feet where it intersected Jade Street. Another long, low brick building, similar to those on Princess Gate, ran from the Fish Pond to Jade Street. This building was also divided into sections, some in ruins and some inhabited. The Clay Elephant was located in one of the ruined sections.

Across Featherbed Lane from the Clay Elephant was a favorite mulberry tree. I'd while away summer days picking and eating mulberries from this tree, my bare feet permanently dyed purple from stepping on the fallen fruit beneath. At the corner of Featherbed Lane and Jade Street was a picturesque two-story brick house, looking like something out of merry old England. It was called the Queen Anne Cottage.

Jade Street ran north from its intersection with Featherbed about five hundred feet where it intersected Hollywood Drive. Halfway up Jade, Frog Lane ran off toward the canal on the east. Between the Queen Anne Cottage and Frog Lane was a long wooden building divided into several residences.

Along the east side of Jade north of Frog Lane was a large wooden building with big barn-like, or garage-like, doors. This building connected to a large two-story brick building that straddled Jade with covered arches reminiscent of the bare arches that straddled Tower Mews at the Clock Tower. The covering of the arches was a habitable wooden superstructure that continued over the brick building as it ran along Hollywood Drive for fifty yards or so. The building along Hollywood was the Thompson warehouse.

Looking north on Jade …

Looking south down Jade from Hollywood …

To complete the Artist Colony square, a large brick wall, more than a foot thick and eight feet high with dark brown glazed clay tile on top, ran along Hollywood Drive, connecting the Thompson warehouse with the Clock Tower.   (The opening in the wall shown below was cut in modern times.)

Growing up I didn't know, nor did I care, why the Artist Colony was called that, it just was. To me the Artist Colony, and the surrounding area, was just one big park, there for my pleasure. I knew every inch of it.

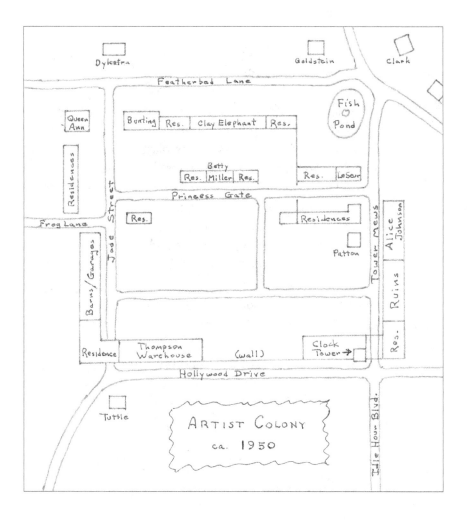

The Clay Elephant

The Artist Colony was a mysterious place. The huge Clock Tower with its battlements was castle-like, but there was no castle. The buildings were kind of connected and organized but to what end? Some of the buildings were inhabited, others not. Everything of red brick, built to last. A very strange place. But we were young and carefree and didn't dwell on the mystery, we just ran around and treated the place as our own.

One section of the low brick building between Featherbed Lane and Princess Gate, near the Fish Pond, was run down and abandoned. The window openings were boarded up, sort of, but not securely enough to keep out curious local kids. This section was mostly empty, just some rubble laying around. With two exceptions. At one end was a huge white plaster cast of two giant men in a grappling embrace, as though wrestling. The figures were gigantic, much larger than life but for some reason were of no interest to us kids. What fascinated us was the other thing.

Near the plaster pile was a monstrous, amorphous mass of clay. It was very large, much taller than a man, bigger around than three men. And it was ... well ... clay. An inexhaustible amount of clay. Clay that could be worked by eager young hands. Grayish-brown and oily, it was permeated with straw-like stuff and hundreds of toothpick kind of sticks that were a nuisance to take out. It was a wonder.

We had no idea what this pile really was or how it came to be but because of its size and color, we called it the "Clay Elephant". It looked as much like an elephant as anything else. This huge pile of greasy clay was a treasure that we mined to make all kinds of things, limited only by our imaginations. I remember various animals, volcanoes, pistols, cars, houses ... Numerous school projects satisfied by clay from the "Clay Elephant". It was a rich natural resource, the secret, private possession of the lucky kids who lived around the Artist Colony.

*   *   *   *   *   *   *   *   *   *

Years later I came across an advertisement for a photograph that looked just like the huge plaster cast as I remembered it.   Here is the photograph and part of the description in the ad:

"Nude Wrestlers"   (1918)

By Walter Hill in the Royal Photographic Society, London

In its infancy photographers patterned their artistic works after historic themes. Reflecting the famous Greek sculpture called "The Wrestlers," the intertwining legs and perfect male forms are dynamically posed in this classic image.

The picture inspired me to ponder the story behind the mysterious "Clay Elephant".   You couldn't tell at the time, because the "Elephant" was unrecognizable, but I believe that it had either looked like the plaster cast, and had been degraded somehow, or it was an unfinished work in progress intended to ultimately look like the plaster cast.

I don't know which came first, but I think that both the plaster and the clay were part of some artist's attempt to create a statue modeled after Walter Hill's photograph which, as the ad says, was inspired by (but oddly doesn't look like) an ancient bronze statue called "The Wrestlers".

Ronnie Loves Mary

Ronnie Dykstra was a playmate of mine in the late '40s and early '50s. He lived on Featherbed Lane in a quaint little cottage that only in later years did I learn was a Vanderbilt Farm building called the Eagle House. Ronnie and I roamed the Artist Colony and the surrounding area as though we owned it.

Among the wonders in the Artist Colony were the ruins just inside the Clock Tower arches where Idle Hour Boulevard became Tower Mews. Essentially the western border of the Artist Colony, Tower Mews ran south from the Clock Tower curving around the Fish Pond and continuing on down to the Grand Canal. Just inside the arches a long, high brick wall ran about a hundred feet or so, connecting them to Alice Johnson's residence. The space behind the wall was filled with charred rubble and debris, remnants of the 1945 fire.

Here's the wall in 1995:

The picture shows a ground level opening (behind the tree) that may or may not have been there in 1951, I don't remember it being there but it could have been.   If it was there, it was blocked off in some way because the only way we could get inside the wall was by climbing through the windows which is what we did.   There were several windows, about four feet wide and four feet high with big gray granite sills.   They were fairly high up, six or seven feet maybe, but that didn't keep us out even though there was little of interest inside.

In 1951, Ronnie Dykstra was maybe twelve years old and in love.   He was smitten with my sister, Mary, who was not quite thirteen.   In those days it was customary for young men to express their ardor by carving their initials along with their beloved's in some tree or other, most famously the "Love Tree" by the Dairy. Ronnie would go one better.   No tree was good enough for him to express the strength of his passion.   No, he would do his carving in stone.   The granite window sills of the ruins along Tower Mews were perfect for his purpose.

But how to do the carving?   The ruins provided the tools. With a big rusty nail for a chisel and a brick for a mallet, Ronnie climbed up into one of the windows and went to work.   Like Michaelangleo sculpting David, he hammered and chiseled his heart and soul into the stubborn gray granite.

In 1995 I took a trip back to Tower Mews and the wall wanting to examine those sills, to search like an archaeologist for the writing that I remember Ronnie carving in the cold gray granite so long ago. The windows were too high for me to look down on the sills. With nothing to stand on the best I could do was on tiptoes hold my camera up as high as I could and blindly snap away, not seeing what I was photographing.   That was in pre-digital days so I had to wait to develop the film to see what I got.

To my delight, I got this picture:

The carving was fairly clear ... definitely readable ... more readable than many inscriptions I've seen of ancient Egyptian or Mayan stone carvings.

And I was brought back to the summer of 1951 ...

One letter at a time, Ronnie labored through the day ... patiently ... unrelenting ... chip, chip, chip ... 'R' ... chip, chip, chip ... 'W' ... 'D' ... on one line ... then an 'L' below and on another line ... 'M' ... 'C' ... And then so that future generations would know when Ronald William Dykstra was in Love with Mary Carlisle, he added the year ... '5 1'.

And at last, it was done, written in stone for all time:

R W D
L
M C
5 1

I've enhanced the relevant carvings …

I was not idle while Ronnie was doing his carving back in 1951. Like him, I scrounged a rusty nail and a brick and carved something in one of the other granite sills.   I don't remember specifically what I carved, I just remember that the process was difficult but that it could be done.   Sadly, the pictures I blindly took in 1995 of some of the other sills revealed no carvings.   They may have become too faint to show up but I'm more inclined to another explanation.   I like to believe that I did my carving in the sill on the far right end, the one where the window has been bricked up.   So for all I know, the identity of the love of my life in 1951 is buried under a brick wall, awaiting some future discovery.

The Sand Pit

On the map Roxbury Avenue looked like a single street running from Oceanview Avenue through to Shore Drive, a distance of maybe 400 yards, but on the ground it was really two different streets. There was a sand pit half way between Oceanview and Shore Drive, right on the line of Roxbury. The section between Oceanview and the sand pit was paved, sort of, but beyond that a double-rutted dirt path skirted around the sand pit and went through to Shore Drive. This section was barely passable for cars. Every now and then, we'd convince Mama to coax Blondie, our '41 tan DeSoto, through the barely negotiable path to Shore Drive. In places the ruts were so deep that Blondie would bottom out. It was great fun.

The sand pit was a special place. How it came to be I never knew but it was different than the surrounding woods and fields, almost alien in its nature. Like another planet. It was very rugged, sand and rocks and fallen trees and shrubs, with mounds and gullies and cliffs in no regular pattern.

Butch and Jody and I camped out overnight in the sand pit now and then. At night it was an eerie place, dark and shadowy and foreboding. But in the daylight, if you were alone, it was a peaceful place, a place of solitude, a place to enjoy a warm spring day, dozing in the sun like a lizard, when there was no pressure or desire to do anything else.

But above all, the sand pit was ideal for BB gun wars. Most of us had one of those Daisy "Red Ryder" models that so resembled the famous Winchester rifle of Western fame. The one that you readied to fire by cocking the looped handle behind the trigger. Had a leather thong hanging from a metal ring on the side, I'm not sure why. What a great gun. Butch had a pump action Daisy that you readied just like you would a pump action shotgun. It was cool too and I think a little more powerful than the Red Ryder.

A number of us, four, five, six or so, would gather at the sand pit for free-for-all BB gun fights. We'd dress up as protectively as we could, in whatever makeshift armor we could scrounge. My favorite outfit was an oversized heavy wool plaid lumberjack shirt and a sailor's hat with the brim turned down so that it resembled a German helmet. The shirt hung down to my knees and was loose enough so that when I was pinged the BB would bounce off without any damage to my body. The sailor hat helmet protected my head, ears and the sides of my face.

Our fights were disorganized, every man for himself. The objective was to hit as many of the others as you could without getting shot yourself. We'd scatter every which way and there were so many places to hide and ambush, the encounters were always different and heart pumping. We didn't keep score. You knew when you hit someone and you knew when you were hit. That was enough.

Sounds stupid in hindsight but it sure was fun and I don't remember anyone ever getting hurt beyond a little red stinger here and there.

Second Pond

Lincoln Drive was a narrow winding road that dove south off a little bend on Montauk Highway just west of the railroad station. There were two or three houses, Marcell's was one of them, near to the highway and then nothing but woods all the way down to the Pepperidge Hall ruins and finally the Great South Bay. Originally Lincoln Drive was little more than a driveway to Pepperidge Hall, the estate of some tycoon of a bygone era.

Well past Marcell's little house, east of Lincoln Drive was a large, natural, fresh water pond, surrounded by the rawest, pristine woods. This was Second Pond. Further south was a smaller, shallower pond. In the heyday of Pepperidge Hall, upon leaving the mansion on your way north to Montauk Highway, you passed by the small pond first and then the larger pond second. Thus the names, First Pond and Second Pond.

Second Pond was fed from a spring at its northern end, draining into a small creek at its southern end. It was oblong in shape, about 500 feet long and 100 feet wide, almost uniformly 2-3 feet deep. The bottom was filled with decomposing leaves and tree branches, the natural debris of the ages.

The big pond was set back several hundred feet into the woods and getting to it wasn't easy. There were two winding, deeply rutted dirt paths that you could take a car through but the paths were not at all car friendly and driving them to the pond was an adventure in itself. Walking in was easiest. In spite of the difficult access, the pond was a popular playground, attracting swimmers and ice skaters from miles around.

The southern end was a true swimming hole. We called it the "deep end" because it was in fact much deeper than the rest of the pond, maybe naturally but probably because someone had dug it out. When I was very young there was an old dead tree at the "deep end" that the older boys used to dive from. By my teens that tree was gone but we could still dive from the little point of land where the tree used to be. For a while there was a makeshift diving board there.

Stretching across the very center of the pond from one side to the other was a narrow band of sand, about ten feet wide. We called this sandy strip the "shallow end" although it wasn't at either end at all but rather in the middle. Obviously the work of man, it is possible that the sand for this band came from the excavation of the "deep end". In any case, it made for a nice wading and swimming area for the younger kids and their guardians.

The northern end of Second Pond was pretty much off limits year round. In winter the pond froze over solidly except for where the spring was. We avoided that end while we skated the rest of the pond at will. In summer we didn't venture there either because of the thick, eons-long accumulation of natural debris. Even the shoreline of the northern end was so heavily overgrown that walking around the pond was nearly impossible and people rarely did it. Conversely, there was a trail around the southern end, connecting the "deep end" with the "shallow end" on both sides of the pond, and pedestrian traffic flowed fairly smoothly between the two "ends".

There was a small round island, about twenty feet in diameter, off to the southern side of the "shallow end" sand strip, nearer to the western bank. This island could be walked to from the sandy "shallow end" with only a little penetration of the muddy, debris-strewn bottom. In summer it gave the "shallow end" swimmers something to do, going back and forth to the little island. In winter it was the perfect site for skaters to gather around a warming fire.

Second Pond was a happy place for me when I was a kid. I spent many hours there, enjoying the cool water in the summer and the large skating rink in winter and the company of like-minded friends and family all year round. We enjoyed many a picnic and weenie roast and skating party and swimming outing at that wonderful natural pond in the woods off Lincoln Drive. We camped and hunted in the surrounding woods. It was just a perfect, natural place to be alive.

And it could have been my grave.

We had been swimming most of the afternoon, my close friends and I, four or five of us. We decided to head back to the bikes that we had dropped at the Vanderbilt end of the trail leading through the woods and across Lincoln Drive to Second Pond. The shortest route to the pond from where we lived, the trail was so rough and root-filled that we always just left the bikes at the other end and walked the last quarter mile through the woods.

With my friends all leaving for the day, I lingered, thinking of one last dip. I don't know why, but I decided to enter the water by what we called a "sailor's dive". Stand with your arms straight down, tight to your side … sort of like those Irish dancers … and dive in head first. It took some discipline not to raise your arms out front.

The bank I dove from was not the normal diving spot at the deepest part of the "deep end", but rather off to one side where the water wasn't quite as deep, maybe four feet. I knew full well how deep it was, or wasn't, but didn't consider that fact when I resolved to do my sailor's dive. So, alone by now, I took my last dive, head first into the shallower part of the "deep end".

Arms at my sides, I hit bottom with my head, pile driving it into the sand. I saw stars. My neck hurt like the devil, and I felt woozy. I was groggy but able to stand up and climb out of the water, thankful that I could. Catching my breath and my wits, I ran after my buddies who were a long way down the path and who had hardly missed me. I told them I almost drowned. They scoffed.

I often think back to that day and wonder why I was so foolish. Fortunately I was as lucky as I was stupid.

The Food Bar

The focal point of Oakdale was the Idle Hour Food Bar. We always stopped there whenever we went out and sometimes we went out just to stop there. It's where we got gas for Blondie from one of the red and white pumps under the big white Mobilgas sign with the red winged flying horse on it. Oddly my mother bought it by the gallon, not the dollar. Five gallons was standard, cost around a dollar ... 87 cents or 93 cents or 1.05 or some odd number like that, I think.

(Courtesy Donald A. Rogers)

When I was very young, the Food Bar was owned and run by a family named Pokorny who were followed by Neddy and Herb Strom, a perfect old Jewish couple. The Stroms had a daughter, Roberta, who worked there too. Both families were part of a tight little community.

I loved going to the Food Bar. There was a lunch counter on one side, a soda fountain kind of thing with high stools where my mother would get coffee and chat with the Stroms and other customers and I would get a small coke and every now and then a hamburger or a chocolate malted.

On the other side was another counter and shelves full of canned goods and paper products, all kinds of sundry things you find in grocery stores today. The back wall was like a newsstand with newspapers and a rack with magazines and comic books, and refrigerated cases filled with beer and soda and milk. In the middle between the lunch counter and the grocery store were wire racks with candy and chips and things like that.

As I got older and roamed Oakdale with my friends the Food Bar became a regular hangout. Sometimes we'd loiter in front of the store, being a little rowdy, watching people come and go. More often we'd hang around at the slight bend in the little path that connected Vanderbilt Boulevard with the Food Bar parking lot.

"The Path", a shortcut through a lightly wooded area, was a natural meeting place for the kids who lived in Idle Hour and went to the Food Bar for whatever reason. We gathered there and hung out for hours at a time, sometimes playing cards or shooting dice when just shooting the bull was not enough.

Bikes made the trip to the Food Bar quicker but as often as not we'd walk so we could search the sides of the road on the way for empty bottles that we could return for their deposits. Quart bottles brought a nickel, smaller ones two cents. We usually found enough for a candy bar and a coke.

I spent many hours in front of the Food Bar, watching the world go by and learning in the process.

The Food Bar was located just east of the East Gate House and back then the big brick and iron fence was still intact, anchored at its eastern end by a large brick and granite column that stood like a sentinel at the edge of Montauk Highway. The column was about three feet square and twelve feet high and capped by a huge round-topped piece of dark brown granite.

I remember climbing this column and perching on that rounded granite cap, becoming part of the column, and watching the passersby. No one ever noticed me, being above their normal line of sight, unless I called to them. It gave me a sense of superiority, being above the other mortals, watching them without their knowledge.

Summer evenings, when the weather was as pleasant as could be, my friends and I would hang around in front of the Food Bar, having nothing better to do, until nine o'clock when Fat Joe would turn off the lights, one by one, inside and out, and finally lock the door, signaling that it was time for us all to go home or at least find some other place to hang out which of course there was none. If there was anything worthwhile going on we'd have been there already and not be hanging around the Food Bar waiting for it to close.

I remember one such night, it was typical, like many others except for one thing. Fat Joe had run all the kids out of the Food Bar and was turning off the lights when Butch's father pulled up in front of the store, got out of his car and headed for the door.

Trying to be helpful, Jody offered advice to his cousin's father: "Food Bar's closed Uncle Andy." Without breaking stride or looking at him Butch's father dismissed his nephew with "Go bag your head" and opened the door and went in. We all fell to the ground laughing, all but Jody that is, who just stood there, sheepish. Funny how little moments of mirth like that stick with you.

We'd hang around in front of the store in winter, too, though it wasn't as pleasant or as much fun unless of course there was snow on the ground. With snow, which we seemed to get more often back then than we do now, the world opened up. We'd spend hours honing our snowball throwing skills.

The traffic going by on Montauk Highway was just too inviting to ignore. Trucks made good targets because they were big and when attacked from the rear it was hard for the driver to see you. Buses were the best; being so long they were easier to hit, and the drivers were reluctant to stop, having a schedule to keep as they did. Unlike cars, buses and trucks never even slowed down when pelted, probably didn't even know they were hit.

We usually didn't take straight shots, there was no challenge in them and being so obvious they often angered the victim, leading to threats of violence and sometimes a chase and a scattering of the gang, which, now that I think of it, did add to the fun.

Lob shots, mortar-like, were better. Much sneakier but harder to pull off. They were a test of supreme skill. The idea was to throw the snowball as high and as far as you could, timing it so that it would come down on the top of a moving target. Without thinking about it, we learned how to gauge the convergence of two objects traveling at different speeds, one on a straight line of variable length, the other on a ballistic parabola of variable height and distance.

There was a lot of trial and error. We'd stand behind the old brick and iron wall on the side of the Food Bar and wait for a victim. The first attempts usually were way off, falling harmlessly behind or in front or to the side of the target. But you got closer and closer, each near miss accompanied by a bunch of "oooohs" until eventually you'd land one smack on top of the vehicle and be rewarded by the raucous cheers of your admiring peers. It was very gratifying.

I often wonder ... What would we have done without the Food Bar?

1958

The Dairy

The Dairy was a place to go.   We called it "the Dairy" because at the time it was occupied by a company called National Dairy Research Laboratories.   We didn't know much about National Dairy beyond the name.   We thought, but didn't know for sure, that they made ice cream.   Aunt Estelle, Butch's mother, had a job there for a while but we didn't know what she did, we really didn't care.   Sometimes we called the huge brick and sandstone building "the Mansion" because we knew it had been Vanderbilt's mansion way back but usually we just called it "the Dairy".

The Dairy was a place to go.   We never went inside the building, or had any contact with the people who worked there, the importance of the Dairy in our young lives was due of the lawn that surrounded it.   Unfenced, it was wide open to anyone who wanted to walk or play on it and we did that a lot.   The place was a magnet for the local kids …   big kids and little kids, guys and girls. Sometimes we just gathered at the Dairy lawn, spontaneously, parking our bikes, or cars when we were older, randomly on the grass, and hang out under one of the big maples or on the hill or the big steps out back by the river.

Often we'd play pickup ball games on the big open lawn on the south side.   You couldn't ask for a better baseball or football field. In season we played both, as often as we wanted.   We never asked permission and no one ever ran us off.   We'd gather after school in the spring to play baseball and in the fall to play football.

Baseball games were unorganized …   We'd choose up sides from whatever number of kids that showed up, if we were short of players we'd shrink the field by making right field foul territory. No coaches or umpires … swinging strikes only …   second foul after two strikes, you're out.   We kept score but forgot it as soon as the game was over, which was usually when it was time to eat.

Football games were just as ragged …   Number or size of kids didn't matter, whoever wanted to play could play.   We played tackle without helmets or pads, collisions could be brutal.   As with baseball, the score was incidental and didn't really matter.

Vanderbilt's mansion was huge. Three stories high, its exterior was red brick and sandstone, the roof was slate with copper flashing and gutters. It was surrounded by a large, sprawling lawn, uncluttered except for a few large trees scattered here and there. The big mansion stood haughtily on high ground overlooking the Connetquot, presenting a magnificent view of the great river.

A wide terrace ran the length of the side of the mansion facing the river. A short brick wall, about three feet high and two feet thick, extended from each end of the terrace, enclosing a large, grassy courtyard. Across the courtyard from the terrace the wall opened to a wide set of stone stairs that led down to a landing at the water's edge.

Two life-size, white limestone lions perched as sentinels on either side of the landing, facing the Connetquot. The lions were long gone by 2002 when I took the picture above but their pedestals are still there.

This gentle hill with its grassy bank sloping down evenly to a low bulkhead was an inviting place to hang out. Sometimes on summer days we'd wind up in the river, clothes and all. It wasn't very deep but it was fun to cool off in. From this side of the mansion you got a nice view of the river and the Arboretum on the other shore.

It was just as pleasant at night, even more so if you were with a girlfriend. You couldn't ask for a more romantic setting ... moonlight reflecting on the river ... soft summer breeze ... it was idyllic. But most nights it was just some guys hanging out, wisecracking or hurling insults across the river at Byron Borst who lived on the other side.

The Dairy was a place to go. I remember especially one lazy day in the summer of 1960 when I was without a car. I'd worked the noon hour at the Food Bar but the afternoon was slow so Fat Joe let me off, not needing me back until the rush hour at five. With an afternoon to kill, I gathered a quart of milk, a bag of Keebler's pecan cookies and a book I was reading on the American Revolution, and strolled on down to the Dairy. I probably knew every one of the nine hundred Idle Hour acres but when faced with an afternoon of solitude, I chose the hill by the Dairy to spend it. The Dairy was a place to go.

The Tea House

A cruise down the Connetquot started peacefully. At its beginning, near the mansion, the great river was narrow but widened gradually as it curved south and then east, finally merging with the Great South Bay. Prominently visible to your left as you approached the bay, on a little spit of land jutting ever so gently into the open water, was a charming little fairyland building that everyone called the "Tea House". The location was ideal, flirting with open sea but still sheltered from the worst of the wild bay.

(Courtesy Dowling College Library Archives and Special Collections)

The Tea House had the look of an English cottage … stucco and brick and wooden exterior with big brick chimneys at either end, suggesting comfortable fireplaces inside. In spite of the robust brick and stucco, it was a graceful little building, petite almost, with delicate diamond framed windows everywhere that gave an open, airy appearance. It seemed almost out of place, this little Tea House, as though it had been plucked from an old English garden and dropped onto this point of marshy land at the mouth of the Connequot.

At the time I didn't know why it was called the Tea House. In the early 50's, when I knew it best, it was a quaint little tavern with a sign out front that said Hotel Pirnat, obviously a place of business. In spite of its friendly, sea breeze atmosphere and perfect location, there never seemed to be any people there. It gave the feel of being closed for the season though I'm sure it wasn't, not at the height of the summer.

There was small dock out back where the water was exceptionally deep, to handle large boats. In those days boat traffic was scarce so the vacant dock made a great place for diving and swimming. At least until August when the jellyfish came in en mass and made swimming all but impossible.

The water by the dock was so deep that we struggled to reach the bottom and get back to the surface to breathe again. There was a nice little beach running away from either side of the dock and we'd lay out on it, sunning ourselves when we tired of swimming and diving. No one from Pirnat's ever bothered us or ran us off, we came and went as we pleased. It was a pleasant place to while away a summer's day.

Then one day Hotel Pirnat was reopened as a more modern and trendy restaurant called Saxon Arms. Probably due to more aggressive management, or maybe the population explosion, business was more brisk at Saxon Arms and more and more people started coming and going. The increased traffic ruined the lazy atmosphere we were used to and eventually we stopped swimming at the Tea House.

The Clubhouse

The shore of the Connetquot River from the Tea House to Snug Harbor was one long sandy beach in the 1940s. Whether it was naturally so or manmade I never knew but it was a pleasant little beach. Ideally located on this beach, between the Tea House and Snug Harbor but closer to the Tea House, was a white clapboard building that looked like a house but was more than that. It was "The Clubhouse".

Officially "The Clubhouse" was a private club run by The Idle Hour Taxpayers Association. A family membership cost I think about $25 a year back then, a lot of money to my family in those days. More often than not we didn't pay to join but since members were allowed to bring guests I usually went as a guest of my friend Butch. If he wasn't there, there was always another friend who was a member so I came and went as though I was a member.

The ground floor of the Clubhouse consisted of two large playrooms, a kitchen and two gender-segregated side-by-side bathrooms. Upstairs there were living quarters for the custodians, a middle-aged married couple.

The larger of the two playrooms was on the south side of the building, the side facing the river. Its three outer walls were all windows, interrupted only by a large glass-paned door in the center of the southern wall. This large room had a wonderful, wide open, bright and airy feel. The only furniture was a half dozen small wooden tables scattered here and there, each with a set of simple wooden chairs. The floor was bare concrete so you could come in with wet, sandy feet although that was discouraged.

The north side of the big wide open room was a large opening so that the adjoining space was really an extension of the large room. This area felt more closed in though, with a stairway and piano on one end, a single window on the other and a wall with three doors on the north side. One of these doors led to the kitchen; the other two to the bathrooms. There was a juke box between the kitchen and the girls' bathroom. A ping-pong table filled the center of this space.

Each of the three small rooms on the north side, the kitchen and the two bathrooms, had exterior doors in addition to the interior ones, so you could enter any of them from the outside as well as the inside. The kitchen was generally off limits to everyone but the custodians as was the upstairs.

A short walk led from the large open room out to the beach which was fifty feet or so from the back door. Some small trees on either side provided shade and a pleasant surrounding for a few wooden picnic tables. Out in the river, a big rectangular WWII life raft anchored about fifty feet offshore was both a swimming objective and a diving platform. A concrete walk led around the building to the rear where there was an outdoor shower (cold water only) that you worked by pulling a chain. The shower had one of those raindrop shower heads that are so popular now and the cold water would rinse the salt off your body and the sand off your feet and then you could go into the bathroom and change out of your wet bathing suit.

We swam often in June and July but not so much in August when the jellyfish came in. In later years, late fifties I think, the Association put up a U-shaped wall of screens in the water to keep the jellyfish out. Eventually they built a dock over the screens so you could walk on it around the entire closed in swimming area. It was nice and extended the swimming season but it imposed a manmade intrusion that took away from the natural feeling of the beach.

When we tired of swimming, we amused ourselves playing ping-pong or other simple games in the Clubhouse. We were carefree … it was a carefree time … we had lots of time to kill and nowhere in particular to go … we were never bored, just very relaxed.

One favorite pastime was the ping-pong ball equivalent of Pick-up-stix or Jenga. If you touch the burning end of a cigarette to a ping-pong ball, it will burn a hole in the ball that spreads until you blow it out. So the objective of the game was to take turns burning a new hole in the ping-pong ball without letting it burn into a previously burned hole. Blow on the glowing end of the cigarette to sharpen the point, touch it to an unburned section of the ball, and blow out the fire before the new hole spreads into a previous one. Nerve racking and great fun.   We were easily amused.

Another popular favorite, although not one of mine, was a card game we called "Knuckles".   I don't remember how to play the game, I only remember what happened if you lost.   The winner got to smack the loser's knuckles with the deck of cards.   Usually, if the winner was kind, or squeamish, he or she would hold the deck kind of flat and slap down on top of the loser's fist so that the pain inflicted was stinging but didn't draw blood.   But if the winner was sadistic, or Ernie Kline, he (or she) would hold the deck edgewise, like a scraper, and strike down on the edge of the loser's knuckles and fingers, scraping skin off both.   It was painful, and left scars.

So we'd while away the summer, one day at a time, and become good swimmers and ping-pong players and "Knuckles" players and burners of holes in ping-pong balls.   We played the currently popular tunes on the juke box, I remember "Wheel of Fortune" in particular, and when we had a little money we'd get a hot dog and a soda from the lady in the kitchen whose name I can't remember. Margie, maybe. Or Maureen ...

Though most of the time we spent at the clubhouse was lazy and spontaneous, the Association now and then held organized events.   In fact my first memory of the clubhouse is a masquerade party with lots of people dressing up in various costumes.   I was maybe three or four and my mother put me in a diaper, nothing else, and passed me off as Mahatma Gandhi.

There were Bingo nights on summer evenings, and dances ... "In the Still of the Night", played over and over, made for a particularly romantic setting.   The guys began to have love interests ... Eileen and Sue and Valerie and Moira ...

Once or twice a summer there would be a clambake that went on all day and into the night ... Steamed clams and corn on the cob, kegs of beer and hot dogs and soda and watermelon ... an endless feast.   People of all ages came and everyone had a good time.

I have many fond memories of those pleasant summer days and nights spent at the friendly clubhouse on the shore of the Connetquot.   I wax nostalgic ... except maybe for the scabs on my knuckles.

The Power House

Most of the streets in the sparsely settled Idle Hour of the '50s had street lights. Primitive, simple things consisting of a flat round metal shade and a bare, clear light bulb, probably about 200 watts, they were hung on telephone poles every hundred feet or so. Not very bright, their light was nonetheless sufficient to keep the lurking night demons at bay.

Central Boulevard was an exception, undeserving of street lights, probably because it was mostly undeveloped. There were only three houses on the narrow street that cut through the woods between Chateau Boulevard and Connetquot Drive: the Trautwein Georgian at the very end of Central where it met Connetquot, the Debus Cape Cod next door to the Trautweins, and a tidy, mysterious little Tudor house, opposite and north of the Debus house.

Across from the Tudor was a massive abandoned brick building, known to all as the Power House. Obviously vacant for a long time, the building was clearly of Vanderbilt vintage, constructed of the characteristic red brick with gray stone window and door sills and the thick slate roof. Since it was called the Power House we assumed it had something to do with generating power for the estate long ago.

The empty building was more or less isolated, almost completely surrounded by woods. The Tudor house across the street was the only sign of humanity nearby and even though we knew people lived there, we never saw them.

Imposing from the outside, the big building seemed even bigger from inside with three levels, one below ground level. There was an array of rooms, some large and wide open, others much smaller. Piles of rubble, some of them ten feet high, were scattered everywhere. All the rooms were connected by doorways to each other and the hallways and stone stairways, creating a confusing, endless labyrinth.

There were things like stages, or docks, here and there, and small tunnels and underground areas that you had to stoop to walk around in. There was one long tunnel that was reputed to connect to the mansion which was about a quarter mile away. Every now and then we'd venture into this tunnel but never got more than fifty feet or so because of the rubble and darkness and fear of bats.

The Power House was irresistible to the wild, unsupervised kids who lived in Idle Hour. We hung out there a lot, sometimes out back among the huge pines smoking cigarettes, sometimes just running around in the building.

On occasion, if there were enough of us, we'd choose up sides and play Ringalevio. The place was ideal for this game of chase and capture. On one day that became special, a friend of ours from Sayville, Dickie Morrison, was visiting us in Oakdale and we were playing Ringalevio in the Power House. Dickie's team had all been captured, he was the only one left, and five or six of us were hot on his trail. We chased him all around the building, up and down the stairs, over the piles of bricks, in and out of the doors and windows. He ran and leaped like a madman but we knew it was just a matter of time.

Finally, he went up on the roof and we all followed. The pace slowed some on the slippery, slanted slate, but we finally had him surrounded and forced him to one end of a small extension of the larger building. He was twenty feet above the ground with nowhere to go. At last he would be caught.

We were within just a few feet when he shocked us all. Turning away, he ran two or three steps toward the edge of the roof and leaped as far as he could out into space.

Our jaws dropped. Like Sinbad the Sailor Dickie flew through the air and grabbed the top of a little oak sapling that rose maybe six or eight feet away, barely as high as the roof. His momentum and the spring of the tree carried him on a perfect arc to the ground, where he landed gently on his feet. Without missing a beat he was off and running, leaving his chasers standing on the roof looking very foolish and in total awe.

We gave up and declared him the winner. Dickie won the admiration of all that day. His feat became legendary and was talked about for years afterward.

One year in the early '50s when our local Boy Scout Troop, #139, was in need of a meeting place our leaders arranged for us to use a part of the Power House. The room in the extension that Dickie Morrison made his great escape from was the perfect size but it was full of junk and debris. I remember spending a weekend with the other scouts cleaning this room out to make it useable. The floor was rough brick or stone of some kind and very hard to get clean but we did it and had our scout meetings there for about a year. We hung a nice hand-painted sign over the entrance to this room, announcing our presence.

The Power House was a spooky place. Foreboding in the daytime, it was downright terrifying at night. We ventured in a few times at night, always in numbers, showing off for each other, pretending not to be afraid, but I remember being scared to death, even with my friends there. It would be unthinkable to venture in alone at night, even if I had reason to, but I do remember a few nights walking home alone down Central Boulevard, the street without lights, past the dark and menacing Power House. Pride kept me from breaking into a run but I did walk very fast.

The Arboretum

"Ar-bo-re'-tum: *n.* A place for studying and exhibiting
growing trees."

- - - Webster's Dictionary

For about a mile of the upper part of the Connetquot River, on
the shore opposite Idle Hour, was a big state-owned public park that
seemed private because there were never any people there. As parks
went, it was pretty boring ... no rides or playgrounds or beaches or
pools, just a bunch of trees and bushes that must have been special
because they all had little signs on them with their scientific names
in Latin and common names in English. The long, official name for
this park was the Bayard Cutting Arboretum State Park but to us it
was simply the Arboretum.

We knew a little about the history of the Arboretum, that it was
once the estate of a rich guy named William Bayard Cutting. He
called the estate Westbrook, a name preserved by Westbrook Farms,
the little place next to the Great River Diner where we used to get
the most delicious whole roasted chickens. Cutting had a passion
for different kinds of trees and he gathered them from all over the
world. When he died he left Westbrook to the state of New York
so that his handiwork would be preserved and enjoyed by the public.
To us kids, this huge park was simply a providential playground that
we treated as our own, just as we did the old Vanderbilt estate in
Oakdale.

There were two distinct sections to the Arboretum. The larger,
southern section, where the mansion was located, was cultivated and
well-tended. Wide expanses of manicured lawns were surrounded
by the exotic trees and bushes with the little name placards along
with pampered native flora. The smaller, northern section was all
pristine woods, native scrub oak and pine and thick brush. The
only hint of man in this section was a rough trail that circled
throughout, marked by a few modest signs labeling it "Birdwatcher's
Walk".

These two very different sections were separated by an estuary that led to a small pond on the other side of the train tracks and Montauk Highway. This estuary was crossed by a rude wooden causeway connecting the two sections. Above the small pond was a much larger one that stretched all the way to Sunrise Highway in the north. The larger pond was several feet higher than the small one, and spilled into it with a sizeable waterfall. We used to hang around the falls, swimming in the ponds once in a while but more often fishing for yellow perch.

Every summer we crossed the river to play in the Arboretum. Sometimes we pretended we were pirates, rowing across the bounding main (the river) to raid the Arboretum, swarming over the cultivated grounds, pillaging imaginary plunder. We brandished swords made from long dowels or broom handles with Mystic tape at one end for a handle and hand guards fashioned from the tops of coffee cans. When we tired of the game we loaded into our row boats and went home, back across the river.

At the southern end of the Arboretum, near the mansion, there was another estuary that penetrated the interior of the grounds. At the mouth of this inlet sat a cozy little island with some trees and a small wooden pavilion on it. The expanse of the Arboretum was ideal for Ringalevio and the little island was the perfect home base/jail. We loved that game and there was no better place for it than the Arboretum. We were very grateful to Mr. Cutting.

River Places

Let's take a lazy cruise down the Connetquot River on a summer's day in 1950. We start at Rattlesnake Creek behind the West Gate House and head south, towards the Great South Bay, several miles distant. The water is fresh in the beginning, getting saltier as we go. On our right is Twin Rivers, a sparsely settled, mostly wooded area with a handful of scattered houses. Shortly we pass Ongania's big stucco house on the little man-made island. To our left is the northern end of Connetquot Drive, lined with a few Burke vintage houses, including my first Oakdale home at the foot of Woodlawn Avenue. Then a long tract of lawn along the eastern shore is dominated by the big Vanderbilt mansion.

Beyond the mansion the eastward bending shoreline is dotted with houses, twenty or more, for a distance of about two miles, all the way to Zaccone's Boatyard. This stretch is punctuated first by the northern entrance to the Grand Canal and then by the little stub of a canal we call Kelchner's lagoon.

Meanwhile, on the opposite shore, the Arboretum runs from Twin Rivers for about two miles before giving way to some Great River homes and a small marina. After that the Timber Point Country Club continues the final distance all the way out into the bay.

Zaccone's is a typical boatyard, providing dock space and marine gas and supplies and dry dock winter storage and boat maintenance and repair. I first knew the Zaccones when they lived in a little white cottage by the Fish Pond, just around the corner from where I lived on Roxbury. Peter Zaccone was my first ever playmate. In the late '40s they moved from the little cottage to the boatyard, fulfilling a lifelong dream.

Joe Zaccone is a happy-go-lucky guy, about as laid back as anyone could be. He obviously loves his work, the boatyard is his idea of heaven. He is a fair mechanic, doing engine work for cars as well as boats. I suspect he never made a lot of money but he is successful in other ways.

Mrs. Zaccone is a friendly, cheerful woman who fits my stereotypical image of an Italian "mama mia" so well that I think her distinctive accent is Italian. She runs a little kitchen in the multi-purpose boatyard building where she makes us hamburgers and hot dogs and brightens our day with her smile and happy banter.

(Joe will die on his dock one day of a heart attack, doing what he loved where he loved doing it. And I learned many years later that Jennie Zaccone was born and raised in Brooklyn, but no matter, my memory is immutable, to me she's forever Italian and I love her that way.)

Right next to Zaccone's is a long, boxy, two-story building surrounded by well-manicured lawn and shrubbery. This is Snapper Inn. Next to Snapper Inn, on the side opposite Zaccone's, the southern entrance to the Grand Canal opens to the river. At this point Shore Drive, which tracks the shoreline behind the houses all the way from Kelchner's lagoon, is carried over the canal by a very high and narrow, rather awkward bridge known to all as the Snapper Inn Bridge. The rickety old thing is so close to the restaurant that standing on it you can almost touch the kitchen where in later years some of my friends will find employment (and good food) shucking clams and cleaning fish and the like.

Snapper Inn is a well-known seafood restaurant at a prime location. The setting is pleasant and picturesque, especially in summer. Patrons come by car or boat for a special occasion or just to hang out. The name derives from the baby bluefish, called snappers, that every summer come by the thousands from the bay up into the Connetquot River. An Oakdale institution, Snapper Inn is owned and operated by the Remmer family. They have a vintage sloop named "Happy Days" that is always prominently moored at Snapper Inn, becoming a landmark feature of this special place.

(Fishing for snappers as a boy from the Snapper Inn dock on dead calm August mornings is one of my fondest memories. More than sixty years later Snapper Inn is still a thriving, popular restaurant, run by an nth generation of Remmers. The "Happy Days", a nostalgic symbol of continuity, is still there, too.)

On the other side of the Grand Canal we find Muff's Boatyard, followed by a stretch of marshy shore and then the Tea House (Pirnat's), the Clubhouse (Idle Hour Taxpayer's Association) and finally Snug Harbor.

Muff's is like Zaccone's, providing basically the same services … mooring, dry dock, gas, marine supplies. They have a greater variety of retail merchandise … fishing gear and boating stuff … and they have sodas and candy and chips but no grill, for a hamburger you have to go to Zaccone's. For a few cents, I buy all the snapper bait (frozen shiners) I need at Muff's.

(A prominent memory of Muff's dock is a painful one. A typical dock with great long planks of weathered pine, I was walking on it one summer day, barefoot as usual, when I snagged a huge splinter in the ball of my foot. The splinter was about an inch and a half long and deeply embedded, going up into the flesh and then back down, and needed attention that neither I nor anyone on the scene could provide. Somehow I got home to my mother and with her trusty tweezers she was able to pull one end out, then the other end, leaving the middle half inch in the deepest part of the wound. Stymied, she took me to the doctor in Sayville who gave me a shot of Novocain that hurt like hell and then he cut the rest of that goddamn Muff's pine splinter from out of my foot.)

Snug Harbor is a typical seaside bar & grill with a perfect name. My mother hangs out there once in a while and often brings me along. A long bar confronts you as you enter. To the left of the bar there is a skeet ball game, to the right is a large dining room filled with simple square wooden tables and chairs. A wall of open, screened windows facing the river lets the breeze blow in to cut the summer heat. At Snug Harbor, located directly opposite the point and the cut where river meets bay, we've reached the end of our lazy trip down the Connetquot. Let's stop for a beer.

(Snug Harbor is still there today, renamed Vanderbilt Wharf, "Vandies" for short. It's more modern but still has the same ambiance and clientele.)

Timber Point

In 1958, my senior year, Sayville opened a new High School on Brook Street.   The class of '59, my class, was the first to graduate from the new school.   Also new that year was a varsity golf team. Now THAT was my idea of sport so I tried out for the team which I think was to consist of eight or nine golfers, with six playing in a normal match.   I wasn't very good but neither was anyone else (golf wasn't as popular among the masses as it is now) so I made the team.   When I played in a match it was usually in the sixth position, rotating with Dufo and Jody.   We had two scratch golfers on the team but the rest of us stunk.   No matter, we got out of class to play golf.   How good was that?

Our home course was Island Hills in Sayville.   We practiced there and hosted other area teams in match play competition. Match play was good for players as inconsistent as we were.   A ten or a twelve that could ruin a medal play round only cost you one hole in match play, no worse than a five or six.

Throughout the season we got to play courses all over the Island, from Bethpage to Shinnecock Hills.   Of all the courses I played my favorite was the Great River Country Club where I caddied and first learned to play.   Built in the '20s and originally named Timber Point, it was a private club in the '50s.   The employees, including caddies, were allowed to play for free on Mondays when the club was closed to the membership.   To us, Monday was "Caddy Day" and we took full advantage.

At first I played with a motley set of old clubs given to me by my Aunt Edith.   She had played as a young woman, many years ago, and when she learned of my interest she sent me up into the very tiny attic of the little log cabin where she lived with Grandmama and Granddaddy.   There I found a small canvas golf bag, barely holding together with leather trim that was all dried out and cracked.   In the bag was the sorriest group of clubs you could imagine.   None of them matched.   The shafts were wood.   These clubs didn't have numbers, the had names like "Cleek" and "Spoon" and "Mashie" and "Niblik".   They were antiques and in awful condition but I learned to play golf with them.   Several yellowed old balls in the bag didn't have round dimples like balls today, instead they had a pattern of square indentations, much like a waffle iron.   They shattered like glass when I hit them.

The course at Great River was perfectly laid out, I thought, but then I was prejudiced, having naturally bonded to the first course I saw in my golf life.   It didn't seem manufactured at all, blending seamlessly into a very natural setting, its eighteen holes weaving in and out among large sections of woods and marshes.   There were a few side-by-side out and backs, like 4 & 5, 13 & 14 and 1 & 18, but mostly the holes were nicely separated.

The course had two distinct personalities.   The front nine was park-like, mostly in the woods, all green and placid and surrounded by tall trees.   The back nine was out in the bay and played like a Scottish links course, all sand and wind and water and tall marsh grass.   Caddying and playing, I walked the course countless times and remember it with nostalgia.

#1 was an easy start.   Medium length par 4, it was straight and flat with the practice range on the right and some very short harmless rough on the left, separating it from #18.   One tall tree in back of the green, no traps that I can remember.   A fairly easy hole, a good starting hole.

#2, a par 4, was across a small service road from #1.   It was very low lying and often played wet, casual water was a frequent problem.   There were woods on the left and the service road on the right but the hole was straight and fairly short.

#3 was a short par 3 surrounded by trees.   The tee was raised as was the green which was straddled by deep traps on either side.   In front and back was steep sloping apron.

#4 was a long and straight par 4 with thick woods on the left and a narrow strip of short rough and the 5th fairway on the right. The green was level and forgiving.

#5 coming back played like #4, only longer, with woods on the left and the short rough and 4th fairway on the right .   I think it was a par 5 but I'm not sure.   #5's green too was level and forgiving.

#6 was another par 3 with trees all around.   There may have been a trap or two.

#7 was a short and fairly straight par 4 but the green was small and crowded by trees and bushes at the property line near Great River Road.

#8 was across the main road from #7.   It was a long par 5 that started in the "woods" front nine terrain and ended in the "links" back nine terrain.   A dog leg to the left, the long fairway hugged very thick woods all the way on the left side.   On the right there was thick rough and eventually a service road.

#9 was a par 4 dog-leg to the left with heavy brush on the left and the service road on the right.   The green was guarded by sand traps.

#10 was an isolated par 4, heading straight out from the clubhouse, aiming at the distant bay, with heavy rough and brush on both sides.   When you reached the green you were well into the "links" terrain.

#11 was level and unremarkable, a par 4 with some brush on the left and sand and short grass on the right.

#12, at 120 yards, was a short but intimidating par 3.   The tee was higher than the green and you had to drive over an inlet from the river and drop the ball onto the tiny green that was surrounded on three sides by water.   It was reminiscent of the Island Green at Sawgrass.

#13 and #14 were side by side par 4s.   Deep in the heart of the links terrain, their entire length was bounded by sand and tall grass.

#15 was my very favorite hole and I wasn't alone in my admiration.   Aptly named "Gibraltar" for obvious reasons, the 15th had a national reputation.   A par 3 of 170 yards or so, the tee was slightly elevated but not nearly as high as the green that sat up on a plateau, surrounded on three sides by cliff-like sandy slopes.   A narrow, grassy, climbing approach was the only way a golfer could negotiate the summit of Gibraltar where the green was.

As a caddy, reaching the 15th was the high point of my day in two ways. Physically because Gibraltar's summit was the highest point not only on the golf course but for miles around the surrounding flat south shore of Long Island. And mentally because with only three more holes to go my day of labor was nearly done. I'd stand tall on the very top of Gibraltar, holding the pulled pin, making sure the flag didn't flap in the breeze and distract my golfers who were trying to putt. The stiff sea breeze coming off the bay could be treacherous to a golfer trying to drive the table-top green but it was a refreshing relief to a tired caddy sweating in the hot August sun. Facing the wide open bay I'd close my eyes and breathe in the salt sea air that cooled my face. Time would stand still. It was exhilarating.

#16 and #17 were par 4s that ran straight along the bay. The sea breeze continued to cool. The narrow beach and bay on the left were always a threat to the golfer. Not quite Pebble Beach but still challenging. The right was just as bad, being rough of very high marsh grass. A ball hit in there was usually lost.

And then #18 turned to the clubhouse. As friendly coming home as #1 was going out, it was a little longer, maybe a par 5 but again I'm not sure.

And the round was done. Clean the clubs and I'd be on my way home with four bucks in my pocket. Caddying at Great River was good. Playing was even better.

* * * * * * * * * *

SCENES

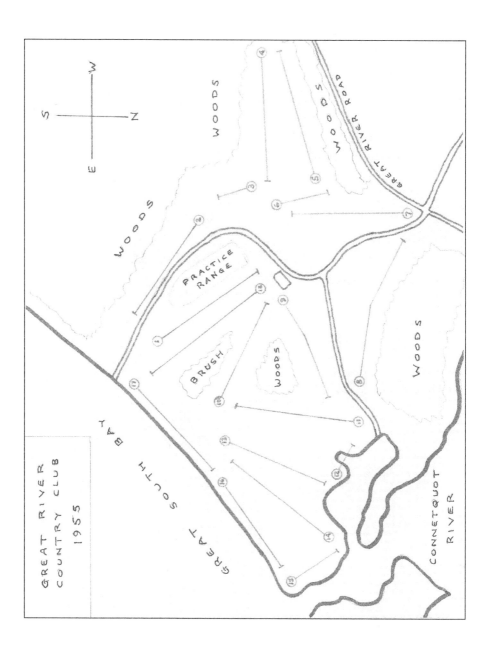

89

*　*　*　*　*　*　*　*　*　*

From the "Suffolk County News" dated May 21, 1959:

Golfers Rout Babylon High

Sayville High's golfers defeated Babylon Friday, 6 ½ to 2 ½.　The summaries:

Paul Sanderlin , Sayville, defeated William Duhamel, 5 and 4;　Ed Belenski, Sayville, defeated Bob Buchanan, 7 and 5.　Best Ball -- Sayville, 6 and 5.

Pat Stamile, Sayville, and Pete Johnson, Babylon, tied;　Henry Hand, Babylon, defeated Jack Bracale, 3 and 1.　Best Ball -- Babylon, 1 up.

Steve Carlisle, Sayville, defeated Lee Mars, 7 and 5;　Bob Platz, Sayville, defeated Tom McLaughlin, 4 and 3.　Best Ball -- Sayville, 8 and 7.

Gas Stations

NY Route 27A was a main thoroughfare running along the
south shore of Long Island from Queens County in the west to
Montauk Point in the east, connecting dozens of small hamlets
along the way. It was generally known as Merrick Road in Nassau
County and Montauk Highway in Suffolk County but each little
town gave it a local name like Main Street or some such. In
Oakdale it was just Montauk Highway. It was the only way into or
out of Idle Hour, by land anyway, and it was lined with local
businesses.

In less than a mile or so, from the railroad bridge in the west to
Stirrup Cup Castle in the east, a distance easily covered on foot,
there were five gas stations, six if you count the Food Bar.

There was Steve's Gulf, Harry's Sinclair, Norman's Sunoco, Art
Premm's Texaco and Tom O'Neill's place that later became Joe
Savino's Power Test. The Food Bar had three Mobil gas pumps
out front, at least for a while. All of the gas stations in those days
were functioning full service stations, except for the Food Bar which
was a multi-purpose enterprise trying to be many things to many
people, a natural, reflection of the time and place and local culture.

Steve and Harry and Norman and Art and Tom were
mechanics all, and while they pumped gas and checked oil and
water and cleaned windshields, they also fixed flats and changed oil
and did tune-ups and fixed all kinds of mechanical problems without
the aid of a computer. If your car needed service or wouldn't run
right, you took it to one of these guys on Montauk Highway.

There were gas pumps at the Food Bar but no associated
garage, not directly anyway. For a time a guy named Ted, a
pleasant man who was married to Blanch Haney, ran an auto repair
shop out of a large garage out back of the Food Bar. Ted drowned
one September day in 1951 when his boat capsized in Fire Island
Inlet. He and two others were coming back from a fishing trip in
the ocean when they got rolled by a big wave. The captain drowned
too but the third guy, who went by the nickname Shadow, survived.

Fat Joe Radgowski who ran the Food Bar in the late '50s was not a mechanic but he was a marketing visionary. The times were changing and he realized early on the economic benefit of a focused mission. He got rid of the gas pumps, and eventually the lunch counter and newsstand, reducing the Food Bar to the deli it is today. Turned out he was right, the deli prospered.

When I was old enough to drive, my favorite gas station was Harry's Sinclair. It wasn't my favorite just because of its convenient location, which was next door to Burke's Log Cabin, directly across Montauk Highway from the East Gate House and catty corner across from the Food Bar. No, it was my favorite because of Harry.

A little hobbit of a man, Harry Mastriano was very short and had a club foot that forced him to walk with a distinctive stilted gate ... swing, stomp, step ... swing, stomp, step. Watching him hobble to and from the pumps evoked Gunsmoke's Chester Good. His appearance never changed ... grimy all over with a little stump of a well-chewed, unlit cigar clamped in his mouth. He always wore the same dark green Sinclair uniform, matching shirt and pants that looked like they had never been washed, and a well-worn, billed cap that hid his fuzzy bald head. The hat was so greasy it looked like leather. His hands, his face even, were as grimy as his clothes and thick-soled shoes. Neither young nor old but somewhere in between, his age was a puzzle.

Harry's speech was as distinctive as his appearance. Obviously city bred, he spoke like a New Yorker, not only in accent but in manner of speech. He pronounced "fil-m" and "bot'-le" as only a New Yorker could. He said "Your mother wouldn't *make* you do it" when he meant she wouldn't *let* you do something. He used "bet" as the past tense of "beat": "He *bet* you in a race."

Some of the more insensitive among my friends would mock Harry from the parking lot in front of the Food Bar across the street ... turning one foot out at 90 degrees and stomping around in a perfect imitation of Harry's limping movement, all the while laughing and hollering. Harry didn't seem to mind, he'd just hurl back some good-natured insult.

The funny little man had a heart of gold. For all his roughness, his lack of polish, he was one of the kindest men I ever knew. If I needed gas but didn't have the money, no problem, pump what you need. He gave us the run of his station … Muller and I changed countless flats in his garage and worked on Muller's car whenever we wanted. My friends and I would hang out in his grimy little office, particularly in winter when it was cold outside and we had nothing better to do and no place else to go. He brokered Black Beauty for me. And he got me the carpenter's helper job with Bill Stiefel. Harry was an unattractive, gruff little guy, but I loved him.

Bars

There were four bars in a quarter mile stretch along Montauk Highway in Oakdale: "Jim's Bar & Grill", the "Oakdale Terrace" (the 'OT'), "Burke's Log Cabin" and "Vinnie's Brass Rail". Bronco Charlie's had a bar but it was in a different category, the bar being secondary to the main business which was serving food. You could stop there for a drink, on the way home from work maybe, and a few did now and then, but this bar wasn't the pub-like hangout that the other four were.

The four true bars were poor man's social clubs, the kind of place where everybody knows your name. They were comfortable places, havens from a stressful world, places where people hung out nursing a beer or a highball, ragging their friends … killing an afternoon, or an hour after work, or an evening … or a whole night … Hell, I "closed" these places many times.

The working stiffs would stop on the way home from work, looking for a break between the pressure cooker of the job and the caldron of home, an hour of respite. There was a common occurrence at this time of day … the phone in the wooden booth on the back wall would ring, someone would go to answer it and one or two guys would holler "I just left". No one was ever there to go to the phone, they always "just left".

Burke's Log Cabin was a little building directly across Montauk from the Food Bar. It wasn't a real log cabin, like the original part of Bronco Charlie's, but rather it had that faux log siding that was used to give a log cabin appearance. Some later owner renamed it the Cozy Cabin but to me it was always Burke's. Vinnie's Brass Rail was catty corner across the highway from Burke's, just east of the Food Bar. It was Ernie's before it was Vinnie's and maybe somebody else's before that but it was always the Brass Rail, regardless of who owned it.

These two, the Cabin and the Brass Rail, were interchangeable, catering to pretty much the same group of regulars. They were close enough that you could walk easily from one to the other, you didn't have to drive, although it wasn't unusual to get in your car and move it across the street when you switched bars, but it was easier to walk. Or stagger. It's a minor miracle that over the many years with thousands of drunks weaving across Montauk Highway in the dark that no one was ever run over, at least none that I know of.

There was a comfortable sameness to these bars. They all had smelly rest rooms and juke boxes and some form of game to play and a grill in the back, so you could get a hamburger or a sandwich. And they all served up the same local beers ... Rheingold, Ballantine, Schaeffer, Piels and Knickerbocker. At least that's what the big plastic tap handles said. Billy Kline, the local wag and bartender told us once that they were all connected to the same keg down in the basement. We believed him because all the draft beer did taste pretty much the same.

Rheingold was special because of the Miss Rheingold contest. Every year they put up six wholesome young ladies as candidates and asked the beer-drinking public to elect one of them to be Miss Rheingold for the year. All the bars had little cardboard boxes with pictures of the six pretty young things on them and a pad of little ballots and a pencil on a string attached. There was a slot in the box so you could stuff it with as many ballots as you had time and energy to fill out. Rheingold claimed it was the second biggest election in the country, behind only the one for U.S. president.

My friends and I wasted many a night at Burke's and Vinnie's, drinking fifteen cent draft beer and playing shuffle board and pool and pinball. We played the juke boxes most of the time with "house" quarters painted with red nail polish that we got from the bartender.

Vinnie's had a shuffleboard and a pinball machine and later a pool table, I think Jim's did too. Burke's had a pinball machine but there wasn't room for a shuffleboard or even a pool table. The OT, too, had only a pinball machine, wedged into a little space between the bar and the men's room.

We played a lot of shuffleboard at Vinnie's, very often for money. Not much, just enough to make it interesting. We were all in awe of Billy Kline who was the slickest hustler I ever saw. Early on he'd alternate wins and losses but then, when the bets got a little higher, he began to win by a point or two. He was so slick. You knew he was hustling you but the games were so close you always thought you had a chance so you'd play him again ... and lose by a point or two.

Usually the interaction with the other drunks was friendly banter but occasionally tempers would flare. These confrontations were typically harmless give-and-take but once in a while they would escalate to physical confrontation and there'd be a clumsy dustup outside in the gravel parking lot. Even those didn't do much damage ... drunks are lousy fighters.

Very often things got raucous without acrimony. I remember one night in particular at Burke's. Reese ("Co-ed") Thomas, a notorious character from Sayville, was really drunk and exuberant. Holding forth loudly he led a bunch of us out onto the little front porch. His car, an older model convertible, was parked right there in front, facing the bar. Co-ed, who I gathered had been a lineman on the high school football team, got down in a three point stance in front of his car. He was really drunk. He began barking signals, and abruptly on his own "hut!" he bolted straight at his car, leaped up on the hood and hurtled onto the canvas top which he quickly plunged through with a great tearing sound. Hanging there in the torn canvas roof, with one foot jammed through and stuck in the steering wheel, his head cleared a little and he moaned ... "Oh Jeez ... my old man is gonna be really pissed at me ..."

It was one of the funniest things I have ever seen. We all went spastic, gasping for breath. I never laughed so hard in my life.

We had some good times at the bars on Montauk Highway in Oakdale.

Highway Hopefuls

In amongst the bars and gas stations on Montauk Highway there was a scattering of buildings where various small businesses seemed to come and go ... insurance/real estate offices, Mom and Pop cafes, marine supply stores, a seasonal vegetable stand, a beauty salon, a gift shop, a one-chair barber shop. These "Highway Hopefuls" tended to be short-lived.

On the southeast corner of Vanderbilt Boulevard and Montauk Highway, just west of the food Bar, stands the venerable old East Gate House. An original Vanderbilt building, it is still a prominent feature on Montauk Highway in Oakdale. (Its sister building, the West Gate House, is not nearly as noticeable because the highway was re-routed away from it when they built the Long Island Railroad overpass. The West Gate house has never been more than a private residence. My grandparents lived there when they first came to Oakdale.)

In my earliest memory, the East Gate House was the office of Mr. James Johnson who sold real estate and insurance. He also lived there. Later on it was the home and beauty salon of Max Tornby, a flamboyant little gay man with a big bushy red mustache. Max had a big green parrot that he kept perched out back of the house in the daytime. Hanging out in the "path", the little shortcut through the woods between Vanderbilt Boulevard and the Food Bar, we tried for hours to teach the parrot to say "Mackie blows" with dubious success. He eventually did come to say something close but we could never really agree on what it was.

Squeezed between the East Gate House and Montauk Highway, there was a tiny one room wooden building, maybe twelve by fifteen feet. I remember it first as Alice Johnson's ill-fated commercial enterprise. She called it a gift shop but it was filled with the oddest collection of sundry things, all kinds of odds and ends, God knows where she got them. Later this little building was a one chair barber shop. In my late teens I went there to get my hair cut, out of loyalty to the locale, certainly not to get a good haircut as the barber was a very bad barber. I was relieved when he went out of business so I could go to a proper barber in West Sayville.

Catty-corner across Montauk from the East Gate House, between the Oakdale Terrace and Harry's gas station, was a long one story brick building. I have no memory of the place until the summer of '57 when an Italian family from North Great River opened a luncheonette there, calling it the Red Checker. I remember the place especially because of the sweet young thing who worked the counter. Her name, Concetta, was as pretty as she was. I'd stop there of an afternoon and nurse a black and white malted and throw quarters in the juke box so I could sit and chat with Concetta. I was really smitten with her but never had the nerve to ask her out or tell her how I felt. My friend Bobby Muller was not so timid, and she fell for him too. They dated for a little while. The Red Checker lasted a little longer than Bobby & 'Chetta, but not much.

Further on down Montauk on the north side, just east of Norman's Sunoco station there was the Antos' building. A fairly large two-story wooden structure with living quarters upstairs and in the rear, there was commercial space on the ground floor in front. The commercial space housed several businesses that came and went, I can't remember any of them except the Hetzel's failed Fish & Chips store.

So far as I'm concerned, pizza was invented around 1947, give or take a year. At least that's when it first entered my world. I was young, maybe five or six. There was a big old gray stucco house near to the train station that a friendly couple named Frank and Mary turned into a restaurant, calling it "Frank & Mary's", I think. At least that's what we called it. I know we ate there a number of times but all I remember was the pizza. It was a wonder, something totally different from anything I'd ever seen. Frank & Mary's didn't last very long but they started my lifelong love affair with New York pizza.

An Army/Navy Surplus store popped up in the late '40s, on the south side of Montauk, just west of Lincoln Drive. It was filled with what the name on the big sign said ... surplus materiel of all kinds, originally intended for use by the Army and the Navy, now no longer needed.   The building was just a little greenhouse, a concrete slab with short, cement block walls topped by a steel frame and glass super structure.   Designed to grow flowers, the little building was cleverly adapted to a different purpose.   The rows of raised wooden beds intended to hold soil and flowers instead were filled with all kinds of surplus war stuff.   The obvious military gear … canteens and mess kits … bayonets, belts and boots … clothing of all kinds.   Unlimited hand tools … shovels and axes … hammers and saws and screwdrivers.   Tents and hammocks and blankets and panchos.   Macho stuff.   This little surplus store defied the "short-lived" rule of the Highway Hopefuls.   Unlike the others, it prospered.   The little greenhouse was replaced with a larger building and the store thrived for many years as the Oakdale Trading Post.

Every summer Sydney Feinberg set up his farm stand right on the highway next to the Surplus store.   It was a large farm stand with a wide variety of fresh produce at decent prices.   People came from miles around to buy fruits and vegetables from Syd.   One day my boss at the Food Bar, Fat Joe, described an encounter he witnessed when he stopped to get some tomatoes or something.   A woman who was inspecting the lettuce asked Syd how much they cost.   "Thirty cents a head" he said.   When she seemed undecided, Syd offered …   "Go ahead, take three for a dollar." And so she did, smiling happily because she got a deal from the hard-bargaining son of Abraham.   Syd was Fat Joe's idol.

There were other highway hopefuls, many I can't remember anything about, a few I remember vaguely … a beer distributor … a lumber yard … a bank … a diner-like place called "The Hut" … and of course, Jacob Jonkers "smoked eels"!   Aah, now there was something to die for.

Stirrup Cup Castle

The Stirrup Cup Castle was surrounded by neatly manicured grounds on the north side of Montauk Highway just east of the Oakdale railroad station. It had a castle look to it but it was more of a large Tudor style mansion. The "Castle" was a popular upscale restaurant with an Island-wide reputation and a unique ambiance. Inside there was a signature feature, a "Wishing Well", which was not a well at all but rather a fairly large but shallow pool of water, with a fountain in the middle.

(Courtesy Dowling College Library Archives and Special Collections)

Patrons came from miles around to dine at this famous restaurant, enjoy the ambiance and, of course make a wish, throwing a coin into the Wishing Well to seal the deal. Every now and then the coins would be gathered with some fanfare and the money given to a local charity.

I don't remember ever having eaten there myself, I think the price range was beyond our means, but I knew about the Wishing Well. I remember clearly a picture in our local weekly newspaper, The Suffolk County News, of two pretty teenage girls dressed in bathing suits, standing in the pool and scooping out coins. I didn't need the caption to tell me that these smiling, attractive young ladies were my sister, Nancy, and her friend, Gerry Muff. The caption also said that the money was to be donated to Southside Hospital in Bay Shore.

* * * * * * * * * * * * *

The Castle was abandoned now, fatally gutted by fire in the middle of one night in the summer of 1957. The building still stood, a tragic ruined hulk, damaged beyond repair, waiting for the wrecking ball and bull dozer.

The night was dark and spooky. Deathly still. A far away street lamp randomly poked little fingers of light into the scene, through the trees outside the wreckage and inside through the disorganized openings left by the flames. With shadows and dim light everywhere, we struggled to see. Three of us, Ernie Kline, Eddie McLain and I, were on a mission, determined to enter the gloomy, ruined shell of the Stirrup Cup Castle.

What was it that lured us here in the dark of night, risking injury, or worse, capture by the patrolling police? The Wishing Well, of course.

We didn't know how many coins were in the Wishing Well but we thought there were enough to make it worth the attempt to get them out. We believed the coins were ours for the taking. Sort of like the salvage of shipwrecks on the high seas. We didn't care that the police disagreed.

The Islip Town Police guarded the Castle ruins jealously, day and night. A daytime excursion into the Castle would be folly, we'd be too easily seen, so we went in at night, entering from the back side opposite the highway because it was more shielded from public view even though we knew the Wishing Well was in the front of the building.

The ruined interior was a minefield of charred remains blocking pathways and crunching underfoot. The pungent, smoky smell of fire was everywhere and overwhelming. Barely able to see, we waited for our eyes to adjust to the darkness. When we could see well enough to get our bearings, we fumbled our way, as delicately as we could, through the darkened obstacles in search of our goal. Our route led us up and down some staircases, the pool being set down low in the front atrium.

The water was black as coal, darker than the night, because of the ashes and charred remnants in the water. Kneeling at the edge of the pool we felt blindly around the bottom with our hands, picking the coins out from among the dead embers and other debris. Denomination didn't matter, not that we could tell anyway; a penny was good, a quarter was great. We put them all in our pockets.

When our pockets were full it was time to leave. We were carefully negotiating our way back up a burned out circular staircase when suddenly a bright light pierced the darkness, focused, moving quickly back and forth through the black interior, creating eerie flashes and shadows. It was the spotlight from a police cruiser that had pulled into the blacked out parking lot. They stayed for an eternity, sweeping the light this way and that, probing the darkness.

I froze, my heart pounding uncontrollably. Finally, the light stopped sweeping, and I, believing, hoping, that the cops had moved on, proceeded up the staircase, one step at a time, very slowly, carefully settling my weight with each step to lessen the noise of the crunching. As I stood on each leg with the other in the air, the weight-bearing knee would tremble, a stark signal to myself that I was scared to death.

Ernie and Eddie and I weren't the only local kids who ventured into the Stirrup Cup Castle, bent on booty. Many others did the same. Pretty soon the Idle Hour Food Bar, the local candy store and soda fountain, was flooded with blackened coins. (Try as we might, it seemed impossible to remove the telltale black stain.)

Fat Joe who owned and ran the Food Bar knew full well where this surge of discolored currency came from. He gave us all a hard time whenever we presented it, threatening to report us to the cops but of course he was just busting chops, as he was wont to do.

We went back two or three times more but the trips became less and less fruitful. Very quickly most of the coins had been taken from the black water and there weren't enough left to make the risk and the effort worthwhile.

And then the ruin was bulldozed and all that was left of the haughty Stirrup Cup Castle was a weed-filled vacant lot.

Long Island

I loved Geography in school. We learned that the U.S. looked like a side of beef and Long Island looked like a fish. It was obvious how Long Island got its name. We learned it was 118 miles long and 15-20 miles wide. Because it was basically linear, we didn't use "north" or "south" very much, most everything was either "east" or "west", or more commonly, "in" or "out", meaning "in" toward the city or "out" from the city. "The City" of course was New York City.

We learned that the island was formed long ago, the "terminal moraine" of an ice age glacier that like a giant bulldozer pushed great masses of earth and rocks down from the north into the Atlantic Ocean. When the glacier retreated, it left behind the basic elongated core of Long Island with its rocky, high bluffed north shore and the trough of the Long Island Sound separating it from Connecticut. Then the weather and gravity and the ocean went to work, leveling and building the south shore and forming the unique features we see today like the barrier beaches and the bays and rivers and inlets.

Naturally, as an island, there was water, water everywhere. Besides the Ocean and the Sound we had bays like Great South, Moriches, Peconic, Oyster, Jamaica; inlets like Fire Island and Moriches; rivers like the Connetquot, the Nissequogue and the Peconic; and numerous lesser ponds and rivers and manmade canals and harbors. And there was the oddity of Lake Ronkonkoma, a solitary, large and extremely deep fresh water lake, smack in the middle of the island, like the big fish's belly button.

And of course the mosaic of bodies of water defined distinct land features: the barrier beaches like Fire Island and Jones Beach, and the peninsulas like Coney Island and Long Beach and the north & south forks of the big fish's tail, Orient Point and Montauk Point

We learned that Long Island was settled by members of the Algonquin family of indigenous people and we studied the thirteen lesser tribes of that family that lived on our seacoast island that was so blessed by Nature. There were the Canarsie on the west and the

Montauk on the east with eleven others in between. These Indians gave us such musical place names as Amagansett, Connetquot, Massapequa, Wantagh, Quogue, Ronkonkoma, Speonk, Nissequogue, Wyandanch, Syosset, Shinnecock, Nesconset, Hauppauge ... and of course Canarsie and Montauk.

I loved Geography, especially when I could live it.

Transportation arteries naturally flowed east-west, following the geography of the long and narrow island. For motor vehicles there was Montauk Highway and Sunrise Highway and Southern State Parkway and Northern State Parkway and Jericho Turnpike and later the Long Island Expressway. The Long Island Railroad carried some freight and mail but mostly commuters between the busy metropolis and suburban Long Island. The LIRR had a hub station at Jamaica in Queens that connected Manhattan on the west to three lines (north, middle and south) on the east extending out through Nassau and Suffolk Counties.

After the war, urban sprawl began its march eastward from the teeming city out onto Long Island. New homes sprang up everywhere, many in huge tracts of cookie cutter houses like Levittown, the development that came to symbolize this surge. The leading edge of this sprawl reached Oakdale in the '50s. That decade, my second on earth, saw my hometown and the surrounding area change from a rural, sparsely populated area to a suburban, densely populated one.

Eastern Suffolk County, the part of Long Island east of the urban sprawl frontier, was at the time still very rural, predominately agricultural. Long Island ducks and Long Island potatoes both had national reputations and this is where they came from. A large section of the shore of Moriches Bay was lined with huge duck farms where millions of the big white ducks were raised. You could smell them from miles away. Huge potato farms around the Hamptons and Riverhead produced potatoes to rival those of Maine and Idaho.

In the spring of 1961 when I should have been in Biloxi, Mississippi, fate intervened and I wound up in New Haven, Connecticut, sent by the Air force to study Chinese language at Yale University. It was a really cushy, civilian-like assignment for a raw recruit in the military.

As the crow flies Oakdale was not very far from New Haven but because of the geography, namely the Long Island Sound, the quickest route home took me through New York City. Almost every Friday night that spring, summer and Fall I took the New York, New Haven and Hartford railroad to Penn Station in Manhattan and then the LIRR to Jamaica where I changed to the southern line that would take me to Oakdale.

Dozens of towns, some small, some big, were strung along the south shore like pearls on a string. The local train that I changed to in Jamaica stopped at virtually every one of these towns, giving me a weekly geography lesson. The conductor would work his way through the train between stops, loudly announcing with exaggerated emphasis on the first syllable of each, the next arrival station and the one to follow …

"**Bay** Shore … **Bay** Shore … **Islip** next …"   "Islip … Islip … **Great** River next …"   "**Great** River … **Great** River … **Oak**dale next …"   And finally, the one that stirred my heart … "**Oak**dale … **Oak**dale … **Say**ville next … " … and it was time for me to get off.   I was home.

PART 3 - PLAY

The idle hours filled

With frolic and adventure

Boredom a stranger

Snappers

In August the snappers would come from the Great South Bay up into the lower end of the great Connetquot.   Not your seagoing snappers, but the baby bluefish that are called snappers when they are young.

Bluefish are a beautiful fish, as generically fishlike as you can imagine.   Picture a fish to represent all of fishdom ...   that's a bluefish, and a juvenile bluefish is a snapper.   And every August great numbers of young bluefish would come up the Connetquot, looking for food or safety or fun, I'm not sure what.

You can catch snappers with the simplest of gear ... a bamboo pole, some string, a bobber, a hook, and some shiners, all attainable by even a dirt-poor nine-year old.   Shiners are tiny little fish, an inch or two long, very slim and whitish with a silver stripe down the length of their sides.   They make excellent snapper bait.   You can catch them in the shallows by hand but it is difficult unless you have a seine.   In the '50s, for a few cents you could buy enough of them, frozen, to last several outings.

On carefree days in August, you get up early, around dawn, gather your pole with the line, bobber and hook attached and wound around, and with your shiners in a small bucket walk up Oceanview Avenue to Shore Drive and then around Shore Drive to the old dock at Snapper Inn, to catch some snappers for lunch and maybe dinner.

The day that would be hot but wasn't yet is perfectly still, with no human noise to mar it.   The river is as smooth as a sheet of glass, without motion except for a pair of ducks slowly leading V's across the water halfway out.   A lone seagull glides above in a cloudless sky, looking for breakfast maybe, or just out enjoying the morning. The peace is palpable.   An occasional "waack, waack, waack" punctuates the calm.

Settle at the end of the old wooden dock.   Unwind the string, dig out a shiner for the hook, flip it out and wait.   A ripple way out, now and then, here and there, tells you the snappers are in the river. The red-and-white bobber tipping up or going under tells you to pull one in.   Into the bucket it goes, with the thawing shiners, and start all over.   Snappers are small, 6-8 inches, silvery-white little beauties. Size doesn't matter, they're all keepers.

The pace is unhurried, natural, lazy.   After an hour or two, the rest of the human world begins to stir, rippling the serenity of the early morning.   And so it is time to go home.   Walk back the way you came, the bucket a little heavier, the heart a little lighter.

Cleaning snappers is easy, compared to most fish.   Cut off the head, at an angle just behind the front fin.   Slit the belly, scoop out the guts, scrape the insides of the empty belly, rinse and you're done. No scales to scale, leave the tail on.   Heat a frying pan with a little butter, bread the snapper with flour on both sides, fry it up to a golden brown and indulge your watering mouth.

Mmmmmmmmmm, mmm.

Bluefish

Pomatomus saltatrix

(A.K.A. - Blue, Snapper, Skipjack)

Barefoot Ratfink

Montauk Highway evolved over centuries along the south shore of Long Island, connecting each little settlement one to the other, spontaneously following the geography. When the railroad came in the 19th century the tracks were laid out on a course roughly parallel to Montauk Highway but more sensibly designed on a straighter line from point to point. At various points along the way, the railroad crossed over the old meandering line of Montauk Highway.

One of these intersections occurred near the headwaters of the Connetquot River in Oakdale, very near the location of Idle Hour's West Gate House. At this intersection, a bridge was built for the highway to go up and over the railroad tracks, so that traffic could flow without interruption. The area under the bridge became a favorite sheltered hangout for a group of curious, active, self-entertaining young boys. Boys with energy and idle minds and time on their hands. That would be me and my friends.

For a time in the late summer and early fall of 1950, almost every day we'd meet and hang out under the bridge, dumping our bikes in the small meadow between the nearest street and the huge overpass. There wasn't much to do in those lazy days. We'd watch the trains rumble by and wave to the trainmen, the engineers in the engine and one or two guys in the caboose.

The terrain under the bridge was a manmade valley, the tracks running through at the lowest level. The ground, steeply sloping on either side, was pure sandy dirt, sheltered from both rain and sunshine. The valley was covered by the huge highway overhead, running crosswise to the tracks. Massive concrete columns pierced the valley, rising straight up from either side of the tracks to support the highway above. The whole was a large, human construction that boasted the power of man.

There was no vegetation under the bridge of course, just hard-packed bare dirt, dirt packed loosely enough so it could be broken up with a little effort but tightly enough so that it stayed together in chunks. We got pretty good at digging large chunks out of the ground, using the big railroad spikes that we found along the track bed, and then breaking the large chunks down into smaller, baseball size pieces that we could throw far and accurately.

We called these little chunks "dirt bombs" though they were more like grenades. It was like throwing a rock only better because, unlike a rock, when a dirt bomb struck a target it would shatter into tiny little pieces flying in all directions. Best of all, if the target was a boxcar the result was not only a spectacular visual explosion, it made a great booming sound at the same time.

What great fun. We whiled away the interval between trains mining the big chunks of dirt and breaking the big chunks down into little dirt bombs. When a freight train rumbled through we'd line up halfway up the hill, on one side of the valley or maybe both, the highway above and the train tracks below. Ammunition stacked at the ready on the ground, we'd wave innocently to the engineers as they went by and then when the engine was past, we'd let loose with a barrage of dirt bombs, throwing as quickly as we could, to see how many pseudo explosions we could create. Then as the end of the train approached, we'd stand up straight and again looking as innocent as we could, wave to the guys in the caboose as they went by on their way to the station at Oakdale.

At first we only targeted freight trains because of the great booming sound and the absence of witnesses but inevitably the time came when a passenger train passed through and we succumbed to our eagerness, launching a few dirt bombs at the more fragile passenger cars. I don't know if we broke any windows but the potential was certainly there and we were obviously seen by passengers and/or conductors who in hindsight we know must have reported us.

One day ... The train was long gone. We were in our "between trains" mode, just hanging out and maybe mining some new dirt bombs when one of us looked down the tracks toward the east and saw some uniformed men walking toward us. Cops!! In a panic we scrambled every which way to flee the scene.

We scattered, six or eight of us, in all directions like the fragments of our dirt bombs when they exploded, each of us taking our own route back to our bikes, stashed nearby in the little meadow. A number of us, three or four, joined up in flight and rode like the wind as far into Idle Hour as we could, to get as far away from the pursuing lawmen as we could, not stopping until we reached Zaccone's Boatyard, about two miles away down on the lower river next to Snapper Inn.

Peter Zaccone was a classmate and friend though he rarely hung out with the rest of us hooligans, he had interests that were different than ours. But it was not unusal to hang out at his parents' place of business, a boatyard mainly but with a small lunch counter where we often got cokes and hot dogs, and we would hang out with Peter, who as I said, was a classmate and a friend.

We were as far away from the scene of the crime as we could get so we stopped there and tried to calm down, pretending we'd been there all day and were nowhere near the train tracks under the Montauk Highway overpass where maybe some kids were throwing rocks at trains.

We hadn't been there very long when an Islip Town Police cruiser came by and stopped next to the cluster of kids hanging around on the street outside Zaccone's Boatyard. Did we know anything about some kids who had fled the scene by the train tracks?

"No officer, we sure don't. We've been here all day and haven't seen anyone come or go."

"OK. If you do see them, tell them they're in real trouble." And then they left, leaving us relieved but a little concerned about their warning. We relaxed a little and after a while went on home.

We didn't know it at the time but Butch Hetzel, after first fleeing in panic like the rest of us, realized he had left his shoes at the scene and went back to get them. Alas, he was captured, the only one caught, the rest of us having escaped cleanly.

When I got home my mother was on the warpath, mad as hell. She knew the whole story and I was in as much trouble as I'd ever been in my life. My sister told me later how a police car pulled up in front of our house, with Butch sitting in the back seat, white as a ghost, while the cops had a long discussion with my mother.

The scene was repeated at Brian's and Jody's, I know for sure, and maybe some of the other kids' houses too. Shoeless Butch Hetzel, the Barefoot Ratfink, had fingered us all.

Wait 'Til Next Year

I was born a Dodgers fan. I must have been because I can't remember a time when I wasn't one.

In the late '40's and early '50's on Long Island, baseball was a basic part of Nature, like sun and earth and sky. It was just there, woven into the fabric of life.

Kids played baseball. Men played baseball. It was the same game. Everyone loved it. We played with our friends and we followed our heroes, the men who played for money the same game we played for fun.

There were three sets of baseball heroes in my world back then: Yankees, Dodgers and Giants. And there were three kinds of baseball fans: Yankees fans, Dodgers fans and Giants fans. Everyone was one of these and only one. You loved your team and hated the other two. And you held fans of the hated two in contempt.

Families were split by their rootings, like in the Civil War but not as deadly. There was no compromise, the lines were clear. My older sisters, Nancy and Mary, were diehard Yankees fans. I was a Dodgers fan. I don't know why any of us were what we were, we just were. Butch and his father, Uncle Andy, were Giants fans. Butch's sister Carol was a Yankees fan, like my sisters.

The names of the hated Yankees roll through my memory, the arrogant Yankees in their fancy pinstripes: ... DiMaggio ... Mantle ... Berra ... Rizzuto ... McDougal ... Martin ... Ford ... Reynolds ... Raschi ... the eccentric manager, Casey Stengel. And the unforgettable voice of the Yankees, the big-mouthed Mel Allen, with his three-ring Ballantine sign and White Owl cigars and trademark "Going ..... Going ..... Gone!" And "How about that!"

You could respect, begrudgingly, bitterly even, the Yankees, because they played the game so well, but you hated their fans, who were despicable. Yankee fans didn't play well, they just rooted for the guys who did, and gloated in their heroes' superiority as though it was their own. They were unbearable, those Yankee fans.

We had some neighbors down the street, the Langstaffs. A nice family, mom & dad, three kids, good neighbors, we liked them. Mary Langstaff was a matronly, friendly woman who happened to be Whitey Ford's aunt. And one day in the early '50s, Whitey Ford, the famous Yankee pitcher, at the height of his career, came to visit his Aunt Mary.

My sisters were ecstatic, and Carol Hetzel too. They had their pictures taken with the baseball god, and got autographed pictures from him and were on cloud nine for a week. What a highlight in an innocent kid's simple life, to meet a contemporary world-famous hero in the flesh. Butch and I were not as thrilled, Giants and Dodgers fans as we were. We got autographs on a 3 x 5 card, no picture. I wish I'd saved it.

Giants fans were fewer than Yankees and Dodger fans but they were just as avid. I didn't like the Giants but I could tolerate them, unlike the Yankees. The Giants were a problem for Dodgers fans and vice versa. We loved to hate the other team as they fought ours for the National League pennant, but when one of them won and met the hated Yankees in the World Series, we tended to root for the National League standard bearer. Fans of the American League Yankees never had to deal with that emotional shift, they could hate both the Dodgers and the Giants consistently.

"Dem Bums" played in Ebbets Field, a shabby old stadium in the Flatbush section of Brooklyn with all those garish commercial signs on the outfield wall. The heroes ... Snider ... Reese ... Robinson ... Hodges ... Campanella ... Furillo ... Newcombe ... Podres ... the names and Red Barber's voice resonate, bringing back memories of summer glory, of hopes raised and dashed.

The Giants .... Mays ... Dark ... Thomson ... Lockman ... Maglie ... Irvin ... Mueller ... Durocher ... heroes to the Giant faithful ... played in the old Polo Grounds, that absurdly dimensioned ballpark with its nearly 500 foot center field.

I saw it in Hetzel's living room on a Dumont TV with a cabinet as big as an ice box and a little 12 inch, black and white picture screen. Uncle Andy, Butch and I were glued to the set that October afternoon in 1951. The game was happening live as we watched, in the Polo Grounds, a sudden death playoff for the National League pennant, forced by the Dodgers September collapse, blowing a thirteen game lead.

The Dodgers were winning, had the game in hand, up 4 to 2 (or something like that). But the drama was palpable: Bottom of the ninth, two on, Bobby Thomson at bat against reliever Ralph Branca. Entire season on the line. I had feelings of dread and remember saying "Oh no, watch him hit a home run", hoping by saying it that it wouldn't happen.

Branca pitching, Thomson hanging in, fans cheering like crazy. The count ran up, I don't remember what it was. And then it happened. The long line drive, the sinking feeling, the announcer going crazy … "The Giants win the pennant!! The Giants win the pennant!! …" The shot heard 'round the world.

I was crushed. Took a long time to recover, but I did eventually. The Dodgers' season was over. "Wait 'til next year." The Giants went up against the Yankees in the World Series and they lost of course. "Wait 'til next year."

Every year it seemed my Dodgers were the losers. Every year summer ended and dem bums again were not champions and all we had left was our perennial response … "Wait 'til next year".

And therein lies part of the magic of baseball, as a metaphor for life. Nothing is final, there is always hope, we have another chance, a new chance to get it right. We lost the game. OK. There's another game tomorrow, we'll win that one. Fresh start. We lost the season. OK, there's always next year.

"Wait 'til next year!" When all the gloating and taunts and boasts and insults had been exchanged, when we ran out of "Oh yeahs", when the games were history, the W's and L's in the books, a matter of record, and the season ended, all that was left was the plaintive cry of the losers … "Wait 'til next year." It wasn't much but it was all we had. The last word.

"Wait 'til next year."

Mosquito Man

The muffled chugging sound in the distance would send us scrambling … The Mosquito Man was coming! We'd scatter throughout the house to close the windows that were all open in hopes of catching the slightest relief from the summer heat that was still oppressive even though it was late in the day, usually near dusk. With the windows all closed and the house protected from the smelly fumes that we knew were coming, we'd run outside and make a beeline to the chugging sound to join the gang of kids buzzing in and out of the great cloud of fog that came from the back of the small truck that was making all the noise.

It was a small truck with a big tank full of DDT in the back and a little two cycle engine not much bigger than a lawn mower's. The telltale chugging sound came from the little engine vaporizing the liquid DDT into a huge cloud of fog that sprayed out of the back of the truck as it crawled up and down the narrow streets around the swampy areas of Idle Hour.

A regular pied piper, the Mosquito Man gathered kids like moths to a porch light as he poked along. The smoke screen was irresistible. Some of us on bikes, others on foot, we dove into and out of the big cloud with abandon, disappearing and reappearing over and over as we flitted into and out of the billowing fog, delighting in being invisible and visible and invisible again. The frenetic group of kids renewed itself, some dropping off as the Mosquito Man got further away from their homes, others joining up as he approached theirs.

* * * * * * * * * * *

116

The wetlands on the south side of Idle Hour, we called them swamps, were very low, barely above sea level. Vast fields of marsh grass grew there, grass that grew long and lying flat formed a spongy mattress-like surface. Drainage ditches were dug through the fields of thick marsh grass, narrow and straight at measured intervals. These ditches, and the intermittent pools of casual water, were ideal breeding grounds for the legendary mosquitoes of Idle Hour.

The state, or the town, I'm not sure which, in their wisdom made war on the mosquitoes. Their main weapon was DDT, the champion of mosquito killers. They sprayed it often all over the most prolific breeding grounds, not only from the special little fog machine trucks but also from airplanes. I remember an open-cockpit biplane roaring over my house on Roxbury, barely above the rooftop, as he turned to go back for another spraying pass at the swamps on the other side of Oceanview. When he banked for the turn I could see the smile on the pilot's face as he returned my frantic waves with a casual one. The sound of his machine was deafening and gave me goose bumps.

I don't remember especially the nuisance that the mosquitoes must have been but I do remember the DDT war against them. The deafening roar of a vintage old bi-plane. And the chugging sound of the Mosquito Man who brought excitement to an otherwise quiet summer evening.

Fuzzy Gray Dot

Butch and I had a memorable BB gun dual one summer day. Not at the sand pit, it was in the field across Oceanview Avenue, along another rutted trail that led through the woods and marshes in the large undeveloped area surrounded by Shore Drive, Oceanview and the Grand Canal.

Just the two of us, we took positions opposite each other, about thirty or forty feet apart, and proceeded to exchange volleys.

My position was almost totally impregnable. There was an old junk car laying on its side in the field. The trunk door, about 4' x 4', was open wide and provided a perfect metal shield behind which I could hide. Even better, someone had shot a hole through the center of the door with a shotgun. This hole was about two inches in diameter, big enough for me to get my BB gun through it and provide just enough of a viewing hole for me to aim through.

Butch set up behind a very large fallen tree, where he had freedom of movement but had to expose most of his head and some upper body in order to shoot at me. We fired away, Butch's BBs pinging off the trunk door harmlessly, mine bouncing off the tree trunk or whizzing over Butch's head, just as harmlessly. What fun!

Pretty soon, a discrepancy became apparent in our relative positions. I was hampered by the fixed and tight little hole, getting my BB gun in and out of it was cumbersome, and sighting through it was restricted. On the other hand, Butch was free to change his position, left to right along the tree trunk, adding to the clumsy adjustments I had to make.

BB guns are relatively weak powered and not very accurate, you can literally see the BB as it flies. In time you can eventually hone in on a small stationary spot and that's what Butch did. His only target was that two inch hole in the trunk door and it never moved. So he fired, noted the hit, adjusted and fired again. Hitting the little hole was inevitable.

I see it still, as clearly as though it just happened. I'm peering through the little hole and a tiny gray dot appears. Fuzzy around the edges, it grows larger and larger. From a speck to pea-size in a second or two. And then pain. I'm hit. In the eye. Damn.

By the grace of God, the hit was not on the eyeball, but a quarter inch away, on the bone above the eye, near the end of my sad little eyebrow. It hurt but at least I wasn't blind.

I still had to worry about my mother. The BB broke the skin and showed a visible wound that she would surely notice and question me about. If I told the truth, the BB gun would be history. So, we made up a story about me climbing on the old car and falling off and hitting my eye on the corner of the open trunk door.

Fishy as it was, the story flew. I was admonished but got to keep my BB gun.

* * * * * * * * * * * * *

The fuzzy gray dot
Expanding, filling the view
Spares the fragile eye.

* * * * * * * * * * * * *

Water World

Oakdale is defined by water ...   The Connetquot River and the lakes and streams that feed it ...   the Vanderbilt canals ...   Second Pond ... the Great South Bay ...   "Water, water everywhere" ... water that was home to all kinds of creatures that entertained and annoyed and sustained us.

In the wide, salty lower end of the Connetquot where it joined the bay, we fished for snappers and blowfish.   We caught the snappers with a bamboo pole rigged simply with a string, bobber and hook with a shiner for bait.   For blowfish all we needed was a spool of string, a hook and some squid.   Both of these tasty little fish were plentiful at certain times in the summer and we caught as many as we could and ate our fill.

Up in the narrow beginnings of the river, where the water was fresh, and in the streams and ponds that flowed into the river, we fished for trout and sometimes yellow perch.   We used fly rods and similar light tackle in a pursuit that took more patience than fishing in the salt water.   These freshwater fish were as delicious but not nearly so plentiful as the saltwater catch.   We sought them more for the sport of it than for filling our bellies.

Second Pond was mainly a swimming hole but had lots of little sunfish that could be caught with a hook, or even a safety pin, on a string, baited with an earthworm.   Some huge goldfish lived in the north end of Second Pond but we only saw them through the ice in winter.

Blue claw crabs were plentiful all summer along the shores of the river and up into the canals.   The easiest way to catch them was with a crab net along the bulkheads where they tended to attach themselves, resting I suppose.   Or you could use a fish head on a wire ring at the end of a long string.   Throw it out and pull it back in very slowly.   The dimwitted crab, focused on the fish head, would follow it back in where you could snag him with your net.   Probably the best (but most expensive) way to catch crabs was to set out a big wire cage trap with sides that closed when you pulled it up, capturing the crabs that were attracted by a fish head tied to the bottom.   All the crabs that were big enough we cooked in boiling water until they turned red.   Getting the flesh out of the shells took some work but was well worth the trouble.   What a feast.

Clams, the hard-shelled kind, were another favorite.   There were some clams in the lower end of the river, but most of the time we dug for them out by the point at the edge of the bay.   Treading with our feet was the usual method.   Very often we'd picnic or camp out on the point, swim in the river or the bay, dig some clams and bake them right there in a fire on the beach.   We lived like Indians.   Of course there were millions of clams in the Great South Bay and we often harvested them to sell at the dock in West Sayville.

Beside the clams the bay yielded all kinds of sport fish that were fun to catch and delicious to eat … fluke and bluefish and stripers and kingfish and weak fish and sea bass.   Unavoidably we'd catch all manner of junk fish that we threw back … like sea robins and dogfish and sand sharks.

Eels are an interesting animal.   They spawn out in the Atlantic, the Sargasso Sea I think, and then head for the coastal fresh water estuaries where they live their lives.   I remember trying to catch the little babies, three or four inches long and thinner than spaghetti, in the shallows out at the point.   There were adult eels in the canals where some of the old timers routinely caught them to eat. Smoked eel was a special treat.

The canals and the lagoons were full of little minnows that we called killies.   Thick set and greenish in color, they made good bait for larger fish.   The best way to catch them was with a killie trap, a small cylindrical cage with an inward facing funnel at one end that was easy for the killie to enter but almost impossible to exit.   Put some bread in the trap, throw it into the canal tied to a rope, leave it overnight.   Come back the next day and you usually had a dozen or so of the two inch long killies.   Just for fun, we would sometimes fish for them with a line and hook with surprising success.   Another way to get them was with the firecrackers we called ash cans.   Put a small stone in either end to weight it down, light the fuse and throw it into the water.   The underwater shock of the explosion would yield several stunned killies floating belly up to the surface.

Some aquatic creatures were common but of no use, like the lampreys and snapping turtles and horseshoe crabs and jellyfish. Once in a while, fishing for trout, we'd catch a lamprey. Similar to eels, these grotesquely ugly, detestable creatures had a big round tooth-filled mouth that they used to latch onto fish larger than themselves and suck their blood out of them. We delighted in putting lampreys on the railroad tracks to be crushed by a passing train.

Quarter size baby snapping turtles were cute and harmless but the adults tended to be ugly and nasty. They thrived in the canals and the shoals of the upper river. More than once I've seen a baby duckling, one of several dutifully trailing its mother swimming in the canal, disappear as though pulled under from below. I was always convinced it was snatched to be a meal for some SOB snapping turtle. The canals being fairly shallow it was not hard to find the snapping turtles and catch them with a crab net. Woe be to the snapping turtle that we caught … his fate was sealed … beheading … for being nasty and ugly and killing little baby ducks. Defiant to the end they did not repent and paid for their nasty characters with their lives.

The big slow moving horseshoe crabs had a hard, helmet-like, shell and a long, hard spike of a tail. The tail looked menacing but I don't think it was dangerous, it made a good handle for picking the critter up if you had a mind to. The underside of a horsehoe crab is really ugly, with lots of squirming little legs. The jellyfish were more than useless, they were a pain. Their sting ranged from annoying to excruciating, depending I think on some mysterious quality of their tentacles. They started to show up in the river in late July, a few at first, but eventually so many that swimming became all but impossible.

Aquatic birds abounded in our water world. Seagulls were the most numerous and as protected scavengers, were everywhere. Mallard ducks were common on the bay and river and in the canals where they tended to nest and reproduce. The ducks were legal game but we rarely took them, their flesh was rubbery and not very good eating. They were best appreciated along with the other birds as artwork, decoration that beautified the landscape.

Less numerous and more beautiful were the swans. These large, graceful white birds were almost always found in pairs, nesting like the ducks in the canals or shallow parts of the river. It was not unusual to see a heron standing at water's edge or swooping over the marshlands.

More than anything, Oakdale was a water world, teeming with a great variety of creatures, each in their niche, enriching the lives of their human neighbors.

On the Water

In summer Oakdale was a lot like Venice ... boats were a common means of transportation. It seemed like we spent more time on the water than on land, going from one place to another or doing something on the water like fishing or water skiing, or just riding around for the sheer pleasure of it. Most of the kids had a boat of some kind, usually a little runabout, sixteen foot or so, with an outboard engine. I didn't have a boat but Butch did and I was his permanent First Mate.

Those were the days before the four mph speed limit was imposed in the canals and the river above Muff's and we loved to run the boats as fast as they could go. It was thrilling, skimming along the surface in an open boat with the wind in your face, feeling like you were going much faster than you actually were.

Every summer for one whole week the river was literally filled with little white sailboats, hundreds of them it seemed like. It was Race Week. The sailboats were relatively small, 12-20 footers, crewed by one or two sailors, in a number of different classes the names of which I knew back then but have since forgotten. They came from all over to compete with each other, to see who could sail the fastest, or smartest, but mostly I think just for the joy of sailing.

Sailing is one of the purest of life's pleasures ... the sense of movement, of silently gliding along ... the wind in your face ... the smell of salt sea air in you nostrils ... the occasional spray of salt water ... no sound, just the gentle swoosh of water on the hull. I've only done it a few times but it is exhilarating. I envied those sailors who came by the hundreds to the Great South Bay in July to compete in Race Week.

The race course was out in the bay, beyond the Point, where the wind was brisk and conditions ideal for sailing. The wide Connetquot River offered a natural haven to moor the little boats overnight. There were way too many to dock at the boatyards or restaurants so they were anchored out in the middle of the river, presenting a great opportunity to any kid with a boat to make some money as a water taxi.

In the morning the eager sailors would hail us from the Snapper Inn dock, or we'd solicit them, and we'd take them to their boat out in the river. In the afternoon they straggled in, exhausted and soaking wet, two or three at a time. Each one picked an open spot in the middle of the river, anchored the boat, secured the rigging and looked for a ride to shore. I think we got a quarter a trip. By evening the water off Snapper Inn was virtually filled with bobbing little battened-down sailboats, looking like a great flock of big white water birds. Race Week was a hectic, fun week that we looked forward to every summer.

There was another week in the summer when things got really busy on the river in Oakdale. This week, instead of the graceful little sailboats, the river filled up with big cabin cruisers. They came from all over, too, part of something called the "Power Squadron". There wasn't any competition like Race Week, at least I don't think so. As near as I could tell, these folks were a bunch of partiers … living on their boats, hopping from one boat to another, they gathered in small groups that got increasingly raucous as the day went on. They had a great time and were very hospitable, welcoming the locals to join them. Another fun boating week.

Water Rats

When I joined the Air Force all the recruits had to be able to swim. If you couldn't pass a swimming test, you had to take lessons until you could.   I was astounded to learn that some of my fellow recruits couldn't swim.   It was inconceivable to me that they didn't know how to swim.   I'd been swimming all my life, I can't remember a time when I couldn't swim.   I thought you were born with the ability, like dogs and cats.   No one teaches them how to swim, they just do it.

(Most dogs love the water and will dive in without hesitation. Cats on the other hand generally avoid the water but if they have to they can swim well enough.   I know this from experience.   Some of my friends worked in the kitchen at Snapper Inn which was right on the water where the Grand Canal entered the river.   There was always a number of cats hanging around the kitchen hoping to scavenge some sea food scraps.   Just for fun, my friends would put some tidbit on the bulkhead and when a cat came to get it they would run up and kick him into the water.   The cat swam just fine but you could tell by the look on his face that he didn't like it.   We all laughed like crazy.)

Anyway, my friends and I all swam naturally, and we did so as often as we could, sometimes with aforethought and sometimes on the spur of the moment.   If swimming was our purpose we'd go to the Clubhouse or Pirnat's or Kelchner's lagoon or Second Pond.   Or sometimes to the public beaches in Sayville or Islip or Hecksher State Park.   There was a really nice little beach out at the Point, a great spot to swim, among other things, where we swam a lot and there was never anybody there.

And then there was the Atlantic Ocean.

The ocean was a whole different adventure.   A ferry ride from Sayville over to Cherry Grove or Fire Island Pines would begin a day of playing on the beach and swimming in the surf.   You'd swim out through the breakers and body surf the waves as they rolled in, at the end of the ride getting tossed ass over head and pounded into the sandy bottom, struggling to reach the surface and regain your footing, all the time fighting the undertow that wanted to drag you back out to sea.   The water was so salty you got virtually pickled. Sand was everywhere and really annoying in your bathing suit. Sometimes you got severely sunburned.

Very often we'd go swimming on the spur of the moment. Hanging out at the back of the Dairy or on a dock at Woodlawn, we'd wind up in the water, no matter what we were wearing which in summer wasn't very much.   Or if we were out in a boat, cruising around, we thought nothing of jumping in to cool off.   Sometimes out in the bay we'd tie up to one of the navigation bouys and swim to our hearts content, miles from land in any direction.

Regular water rats, we were.

Ice Capades

"es'-ca-pade: *n.*   A playful or reckless adventure."

- - - Webster's Dictionary

The waterways of Oakdale, so much a part of our lives as playgrounds and thoroughfares in spring and summer and autumn, did not withdraw as such when winter came.   Hardened by nature, they were still our playgrounds and thoroughfares.

The little Fish Pond in the Artist Colony, home to frogs and goldfish and water lilies in warm weather, was early to freeze over. It was in the Fish Pond's friendly, close-to-home confines that I was introduced to ice skating when I was very young, maybe four or five years old.   My first skates were simple little double-bladed things that strapped on to my shoes, like those old roller skates you tightened with a key.   In time I graduated to my sister's hand-me-down figure skates, shrugging off the humiliation of their white color.   Skating was pure fun, the color of the boot had no effect on function.

Also early to freeze was the little swamp across Shore Drive from the big white house where the Sosnilos and Von Der Vors lived when they first came to Oakdale.   The few inches of casual water froze readily, becoming a useable but tricky little rink that served until the larger venues froze over.   Skating on this little swamp was complicated by all the weeds and stuff stuck in the ice.   Valerie Powell broke her leg skating here one year.

Second Pond was one of the larger venues and very popular. Relatively shallow and with fresh water it was quick to freeze over too … all except for the northern end where the spring was, this area was open all winter and we gave it a wide berth.   Well known as a swimming hole, Second Pond attracted skaters from miles around.   The lone little island was the perfect place for a warming fire.

A local family on Second Pond ca. 1955 …

The Vanderbilt canals and their lagoons, being slightly brackish and deeper than the ponds and the little swamp, took longer to freeze over.   We tested them daily, first by throwing out the biggest rocks or bricks or logs that we could find and then by venturing out carefully, to see if the ice would hold.   Once thick enough, the ice usually lasted through the winter and we skated every day on one or more of the lagoons … Clamsers' or Parringtons' or Kelchners' or Borsts'.   Clamsers' was a favorite because we could warm up in Aunt Helen's house and in later years Aunt Mary's after the Von Der Vors moved next door to the Clamsers.

Valerie on the Clamser Lagoon ca. 1960 …

The lagoons, oval shaped and the perfect rink size, were the hubs of activity where groups of skaters gathered to enjoy the sport and practice their moves and show them off, some more accomplished than others, all having a good time.   'Round and 'round as fast as you can go, "Crossing the Bar" or "Cracking the Whip".   Or slowly gliding around, relaxed and effortless, utterly carefree.

If there were enough of us we'd choose teams and play a ragged pick-up game of hockey.   We had no equipment other than our skates.   Tree branches taken out of the nearby woods became hockey sticks, a little piece of wood made a good puck, and two cans or rocks or bricks or hats set a few feet apart at either end served as goals.   And the game was on.

The canals linked the lagoons and the river and we skated on them to get from one to another or just to escape the bustle of the lagoons.

The best of all was the Connetquot River, especially at the upper end where the freshwater ice was clear and dark, almost black, so transparent it was scary.   Smooth as glass it was, before the snow came and messed it up.   In daytime you could see through to the river bottom.

At night skating on the river was a glorious, exhilarating experience ...   Gliding along, no sound save the whisper of the blades slicing over the smooth dark ice ... the air crisp and pure ... cold enough to make you feel alive ... suspended in time ... borne like a feather on the breath of God ... the stars like diamonds in the pitch black sky.   It was spiritual.

The lagoons and ponds were good rinks but they had limits, you had to skate in circles.   On the river you could skate for miles in a straight line, turning or stopping only when you got tired.   You were free as a bird in the sky.

A sketch of the Vanderbilt Tea House on a winter day, the frozen river behind …

(Courtesy Dowling College Library Archives and Special Collections)

Skating on the river could be scary, too.   One day in mid-winter, Butch and I were out on the river that was frozen all the way to the bay.   We were on the Great River side, across from Muff's and heading out toward the Timber Point "cut".   The ice at this end of the river was opaque, white, because of the salt in it I guess. We were moving along at a good clip, Butch ahead of me by thirty yards or so, when I noticed a waving motion of the ice in front of me.   Butch was in a trough, a depression, that moved with him as he skated forward.   Behind him was a rise that I realized must be between his trough and another that was mine.   Not very solid, I remember thinking.   Then when my skate blade punctured the ice as I pushed forward, I realized how precariously thin the ice must be.

With a shudder I thought that our speed was the only thing keeping us from falling through the ice, an event that could have been very serious.   Without slowing down, I hailed Butch and convinced him to follow me back to where we had come from.

Now that was an "ice capade".

Captain Borst

It was a Saturday in November, one of those late Fall days when you know that it's not yet winter but summer is long gone. Gray and cool, a crummy day to most people, weather-wise anyway. But to a group of young Boy Scouts on a boating adventure it was a fine day.

We left early in the morning, bound for a tour of the grand Fire Island Lighthouse. Two boatloads of Scouts and their leaders, out of Oakdale down the Connetquot River, through the Timber Point "cut" and across Great South Bay to Fire Island Inlet where the famous lighthouse stood at the western end of Fire Island.

On board the larger of the two boats, a 40-foot cabin cruiser belonging to Bill Newhouse, Sr., were a dozen or so of the older Scouts of Troop 139, and three or four leaders. The smaller boat, *Lois III*, was a 28-foot Chris Craft cabin cruiser owned and captained by Byron T. Borst, Sr. *Lois III* carried a half dozen or so of the younger scouts; Captain Borst was the lone leader.

From the Grand Canal in Idle Hour, where *Lois III* was moored, the hour-long trip down the river and across the bay was uneventful. At our destination, we couldn't go into the lighthouse but we ran all around it and the surrounding sandy barrier beach, from the bay side to the ocean side. Swimming was out of the question but most of us romped in the ocean surf and got our clothes wet enough to make us uncomfortable in the raw November air.

The outing thus far was enjoyable but the real fun started on the trip back. The two boats left for home at the same time. Just under way, Captain Borst declared something like "Let's beat 'em home, boys!" and took a diagonal across the bay, a beeline to the "cut" while Captain Newhouse took the normal route, parallel to Fire Island before making a 90 degree turn to the "cut". Since we were taking the shortest line, surely we would beat them by a mile.

Before long, as we raced across the water, those of us watching off the back of the boat noticed some mud churning up. "Mr. Borst, Mr. Borst," Butch shouted, "We're running aground!"

"So we are," our Captain replied with calm assurance. "Don't worry, boys, it's just a sand bar, we'll run right over it" and he gunned the engine. The engine struggled but the boat slowed, until she barely moved. Finally Captain Borst proclaimed: "Looks like we can't get over it, after all. Don't worry, boys, we'll just back off and go around." Whereupon he threw *Lois III* into reverse and gunned the engine some more. More noise, more mud, but less and less movement. Forward again, then backward, and forward again. It seemed like we were digging a nice little hole to settle in. And we were stuck. No matter how hard Captain Borst coaxed her, *Lois III* finally wouldn't budge.

Captain Borst, God love him, was a confident and optimistic man. He pondered. "I've got it! We'll throw the anchor out and we'll all pull our ship right off this cursed little sand bar." Good idea. He tossed the anchor out, as far as he could and we all grabbed hold of the rope and pulled for all we were worth. And we pulled. And pulled. Not an inch. The boat was stuck, and the anchor was now permanently embedded in the bottom of the bay. Well, at least we wouldn't drift away, since we were firmly anchored.

Captain Borst pondered some more. What to do? ... Aha! "We'll get out and push!"

The water was only three feet deep or so and he thought we could muscle the boat off the sand bar if we could get our shoulders into it. So he went to the stern and, not wanting to get his pants wet, he shed them and, wearing nothing but a shirt, faced his young crew and appealed for volunteers: "What brave Boy Scout is going to help me push the boat off this sand bar?"

Well, it was November in New York, and having had a dose of the ocean on Fire Island, these Boy Scouts were more pragmatic than brave. No one stepped up. "Well then, I'll do it by myself" he declared. He stretched one leg out over the stern and, hairy ass mooning us to our glee, he tested the water. "Whooooa! .... On second thought, I don't think this will work either."

So he put his pants back on and pondered some more. Finally, he says "Don't worry, boys. The tide is coming in, we'll just wait a while and the water will lift us off of this little sand bar and we'll be on our way."

By now, the Newhouse boat was long out of sight and we had no hope of beating them home. In fact, we'd be glad just to get home.

And so we waited, not very worried and still having a great time.

But we were getting hungry. And thirsty. There were few provisions on board *Lois III*, it was supposed to be just a day trip after all. We did have some water and powdered Cocoa and a small alcohol stove. Captain Borst decided to make some hot Cocoa for us to drink while we waited for the tide to come in. He fired up the little stove and put some water on to boil.

By now the more observant of us began to suspect that rather than "coming in" as our Captain had told us, the tide was in fact "going out." Our suspicions were confirmed by a noticeable list to starboard. So, it looked like we were not going to be floated off very soon. Worse, the list had caused a spilling over of the alcohol in the little stove, and of a sudden there was fire on the adjacent counter top. "Mr. Borst!, there's fire!"

The Captain leaped into action. "Stand back, boys!" He grabbed the pot of boiling water and with authority doused the burning alcohol. Whew, that was close. The fire was out and we were saved. Disaster averted. But alas, now the water was gone and there would be no hot Cocoa this night. Oh well, small price to pay for being alive.

Soon the sun set, the tide continued to go out and the list became worse. We resolved to await rescue or the returning tide, whichever came first. There were bunks on the *Lois III* but even though we tried to rest in them, it was impossible because of the steep angle of the list. You either rolled out or were smashed up against the bulkhead, depending on which side you chose.

Night fell. It was pitch dark. To pass the time and thinking it was the clever scouting thing to do, we took turns using the little interior dome light to flash SOS in Morse code, to guide the rescuers who surely were searching the bay for the lost scouts. Short-short-short, long-long-long, short-short-short. We were proud we knew the code. This pretty quickly became tedious and we gave it up.

After an eternity, probably several hours, we heard men's voices from the dark across the water to the southeast, "hallooing" kinds of shouts. We were saved! And then there was Rusty Muff in a row boat. The little boat had an outboard motor but the water by now was so shallow, about a foot deep, that the outboard was unusable and Rusty had to row.

Rusty had come from a larger craft, one of several including the Coast Guard, out searching for the lost scouts of Troop 139. It may have been the Newhouse boat but I think it was another, Tony Leis' *El-Ant* or Rusty's boat or his father's or some other good Samaritan's. In any case, she was standing by about half a mile from *Lois III*, prevented from approaching any closer by the shallowness of the water. Our boat was firmly aground, well into that area of Great South Bay east of East Island called "the flats." This area was inviting as a short cut but was wisely avoided by most sailors.

The weary but happy scouts were quickly transferred to Rusty's small row boat, then to the larger craft and back through the dark night to Muff's Boatyard in Oakdale. There we were met by a crowd of very anxious but relieved parents and other family and friends. My worried mother was among them and I was glad to see her but not nearly as glad as she was to see me. The group was pretty emotional. What had been a lark to us kids was a nightmare to those who loved us and didn't know where we were, lost at sea. Their horrible imaginings never occurred to us.

Mr. Borst, good Captain to the end, stayed on board the grounded, listing *Lois III*. The next day, with the returning tide, he and his craft were pulled off the cursed flats and they both returned safely to their Idle Hour home. "All's well that ends well." It was a most memorable day.

* * * * * * * * * * * * * *

* * * * * * * * * * * * * *

    I am challenged to construct a list of the scouts on board Lois III *that day. My dilemma is two kinds of memories. I have "original" memories, visions in my mind that I can clearly and directly connect in real time with actual happenings. And I have "conjured" memories, visions reasonably inferred from the context of the events. Over time, these latter are recycled as recalled memories along with the former and the two become harder to tell apart. Memories of memories become memories unto themselves, regardless of their origin.*

    I have very clear "original" memories only of Butch Hetzel and Peter Zaccone, besides of course Captain Borst and myself. I have not so clear yet still "original" memories that lead me to believe in the presence of two others: David Van Weele and Kenny Langstaff. I believe these two must have been there because neither was a close friend and I would have no reason to "conjure" their memory. I do "conjure" the presence of three others: Byron Borst, Jr., since he was a scout and it is inconceivable that he would not accompany his father on that outing, and Jody Von Der Vor and Brian Van Weele, because they, Butch and I were inseparable in those days.

    So that makes eight scouts and the Captain. Not an unreasonable number, but near the limit for Lois III *and a lone leader. Oh, yeah, the year was early '50s, probably '53 or '54.*

Kon Tiki

In summer, when school let out, we'd shed shoes and shirts and live like Indians until September. The soles of our feet got rock-hard and our exposed bodies tanned brown as berries. We swam nearly every day in pond, canal, lagoon, river, bay or ocean. We led a carefree existence.

One summer, 1954 I think, large groups of us, 10 or 12 or 15 teenage boys, hung out around Kelchner's lagoon a lot. Almost every day we'd gather to swim and frolic in the lagoon and canal behind Kelchner's house down on Shore Drive.

One thing we loved to do was swamp boats. As many of us that could fit would load up into a row boat that we'd take out to the middle of the lagoon and sink and re-float and sink again, over and over. Eventually we tired of that game and conspired to try something more ambitious.

We divided into teams of three, each team with the objective of building some kind of boat, from whatever material they could come up with, and see who could build the best boat.

I only remember two of the teams ... my own, made up of Billy Kelchner, Everett Och and me, and one other including Butch Hetzel, Billy Newhouse and Phil Olivier, Newhouse's step brother. I remember the Newhouse team because they decided to build a submarine and we all thought they were nuts.

My team chose to build a raft, probably because we knew of a great big jumbled pile of large pine logs on the shore across the river over by the wild section of the Arboretum, half in and half out of the water, refuse from some land clearing operation.

These were large pine logs, straight and long, 8-10 inches in diameter. They were too heavy to lift but once in the water they could be managed easily enough. We must have had to cut them to length but I don't remember doing that. What I do remember is winding up with four or five logs, 12-14 feet long, that we lashed together to form the center of our raft. Then we took six more, 8-10 feet long and lashed three each to either side of the longer set, ends flush at the rear to form a rectangular log platform with a nice little 3' x 3' prow jutting out from one end.

We floated the basic raft back across the river to Kelchner's lagoon where we finished it off. Billy had some scrap lumber in his back yard, including some sheathing and an old, white, cross-shaped mast that may have been a flag pole, I'm not sure. We attached the big cross-shaped mast securely to the front center of the raft. Then we nailed the sheathing across the logs to form a nice smooth deck. A poncho acquired from the Army-Navy surplus store made a perfect sail (except for the little hole in the middle).

When it was finished, the thing looked like Kon Tiki. It was very impressive. The raft was so massive that the three of us could stand and run around on it and it barely moved.

It wasn't the most graceful of crafts but it floated nicely and we could maneuver it pretty well with paddles, albeit slowly. When we got her out in the river and unfurled the sail, a little breeze would move the thing along fast enough so we didn't have to paddle, we could just lounge on the deck and enjoy the day and the ride. Regular Huck Finns, we were.

Only bad thing was, our Kon Tiki with its square-rigged, fixed sail, would only sail with the wind, so after the easy ride downwind, we'd have to furl the sail and paddle her back. This was a little tedious but we weren't smart enough to resolve the problem.

The other boat-building groups progressed to varying degrees but eventually all failed, our raft was the only usable craft produced. Thank God the submarine builders never got close enough to anything they could try out, they'd have drowned for sure.

We used Kon Tiki the rest of the summer, sometimes for rides in the river but more often as a diving and lounging platform for swimming in Kelchner's lagoon, which, as I said, we did a lot that year.

When Fall came the big raft was way too heavy to take out of the water so she stayed moored in the canal behind Kelchner's house all winter. By the following spring she was water-logged and pretty much sunk, certainly not seaworthy. I don't remember her final demise, probably disassembled and the parts allowed to sink or float away. She lives on only in memory.

Last Outing

Snowflakes, not many, not big, but very obviously snowflakes, were falling gently, clinging to my sleeping bag where they fell that November morning in 1955.   I knew when I saw snow that this was the last outing of the season.   It was entirely too cold to be sleeping on the ground out in the woods.   My friends and I enjoyed the freedom from adults that "camping out" gave us but there comes a time when it's not worth it.   For sure this was our last outing, we'd be spending nights at home from now on, at least until spring.

The air was gray and dreary and cold, tiny snowflakes spitting on and off throughout the day.   An uncomfortable day, I've recalled it many times through the years.   Whenever I go out on a late autumn or winter day wearing just a T-shirt, usually to get the paper or the mail, and feel the chill in the air to the point of pain, I remember that November day, the day of the last outing.   And I think of Larry Race on the beach.

They found him about 11 that night, no shirt, no shoes, on the bay side beach of Fire Island.   He'd been dead only an hour or two, dying from exposure that cruel, cold night.   Further on down the beach they found the cabin cruiser, run aground, throttle wide open.

There was no sign of Pete Sprague, Larry's companion on that outing.   They searched through the night and all the next day. Come daylight they found the little duck boat the two had taken with them, half sunk out in the bay, not far from where the larger boat was beached.   For several days they dragged the bay until finally a grappling hook caught Pete's submerged body in the eye socket and the search was over.

The two fifteen year olds had left that morning, very early, to go duck hunting on the Great South Bay.   They went in a cabin cruiser, belonging to one of their parents, I don't remember which, and brought along one of those little gray, canvas duck boats that I assume they planned to use in some shallows where they would set up to wait for the ducks.

Pete and Larry were a year ahead of me in school, I knew them mostly from a gun safety class we had attended together earlier that Fall. The class was required in order to get a hunting license. They were responsible young men, obviously trusted to go out by themselves in a large cabin cruiser on the Great South Bay which is a very large body of water. But something went wrong.

It was impossible to say for sure what happened that day. We could only imagine. Obviously the larger boat, perhaps pilotless, ran aground under power onto Fire Island. How did Pete and Larry wind up in the water? Did they both go overboard at the same time? Or did one go over first and the other when he tried to get back to him or in an attempt to get to shore? Was there some accident that caused one or both to go overboard? Were they fooling around? Were they fighting? Why was the little duck boat sunk? What happened to Pete, the better athlete, that kept him from shore? How far did Larry have to swim?

We'll never know. We only know they died way too young. And now every time I go scantily clad out into the cold I think of Larry Race and how he must have suffered, shivering in the cold air, reaching the beach with his last ounce of strength, conscious but too weak to move any further, then losing consciousness, never to wake up.

* * * * * * * * * * * * *

Cold gray autumn day
Two young hunters on the bay
On the last outing

* * * * * * * * * * * * *

* * * * * * * * * * * * *

I wrote "Last Outing" fifty years after the event based solely on my memory of it.   Since writing the memoir I have learned more about the tragedy from other sources, namely contemporary Suffolk County News reports and accounts from classmates drawing on their memories as I did.   My memory had a few of the details wrong and of course it was from my own narrow perspective but it essentially agrees with the Suffolk County News reports.

The story was a huge one back in November 1955.   Sayville was a small, close-knit community.   Pete Sprague's father was a Fire Chief with the Sayville Fire Department.   The Races, relative newcomers from Nassau County, were apparently well known and respected.   Larry and Pete were popular Sayville High School athletes, at fifteen in the prime of their lives.

It was a Saturday morning, November 19, 1955, and the two teenagers planned a day of duck hunting on the bay.   At 5:30 a.m., Larry's father, Cecil, watched them head out in his 30-foot cabin cruiser, the Lazy Legs, towing a small duck boat behind.   They were to return at noon.   In the pre-dawn the sky was clear and the bay was calm but later in the morning the weather turned as I remembered it ...   gray and cold with intermittent snow and sporadic winds.

As the afternoon wore on and the boys didn't come home the parents became increasingly concerned.   Around 4 p.m. Cecil Race and Chief Sprague both called the Coast Guard to report the boys missing and to ask them to conduct a search.   Chief Sprague also called the Islip and Brookhaven police.   And then they waited ... and worried.   Several calls to the Coast Guard throughout the evening were fruitless.

Finally, discouraged by the Coast Guard's seeming ineffectiveness, the Chief acted.   Gathering lights, blankets and other emergency equipment from the Sayville Fire House, *"Chief*

Sprague, accompanied by Dr. Peter Lerner and Fred Dioquardo of Bayport, an uncle of the Sprague youth, borrowed a small skiff from Jack Lembeck ... and rode to the beach in a howling snowstorm ... arriving at Fire Island Pines at 11:15". [1]   There they were *"joined by a party of ... local men who were aboard a private boat owned by Richard Brennan and moored in the Fire Island Pines basin."* [2]   Besides Brennan, this group *"included William Schaper, Wilber Prall, Ed Kinkaide, John Griek, and Dr. Ed Smith."* [3]

The searchers set out on foot to find what had appeared to be a cruiser up against the shore that they had seen while en route to the basin at Fire Island Pines.   *"The 30 foot cabin cruiser ... was found at about 1:30 a.m. Sunday at Fisherman's Path, a half mile east of Fire Island Pines.   The boat was hard aground in shoal water about 150 feet from the beach, its running lights still on and its engine in gear but stalled.   The Race boy's body was lying face down in the freezing water close to the grounded craft.   ...   He was pronounced dead by Dr. Lerner ... Later it was determined that (he) had died of drowning and exposure.   The searchers then began a frantic hunt for the Sprague boy but could find no trace of him or of the eight foot wooden punt ... nor ... any trace of the boys' guns.   They walked along the bayfront, in the teeth of strong northeast wind and driving snow, throughout the night, but in vain.   Several plastic and wooden duck decoys were found drifting near the beach."* [4]

"Shortly after dawn Sunday a Coast Guard helicopter arrived and began a systematic search of the area.   It combed the entire waterfront, only a few feet above the water, and cruised inland at low level.   Later in the morning Civil Air Patrol planes and a Coast Guard Auxiliary vessel joined the search and at 11 a.m. a chartered Cherry Grove Ferry Service vessel arrived at Fire Island Pines carrying 60 members of the Sayville Fire Department and other volunteers summoned together by First Assistant Chief Charles Suckow.   The fireman fanned out in a thorough search of the beach area.   They covered the bayfront foot by foot from Leja Beach west to Point O'Woods and combed through wooded areas and looked into vacant

---

[1] "Two Boys Lost in Bay", *Suffolk County News*, November 25, 1955
[2] Ibid
[3] "Coast Guard is Panned", *Suffolk County News*, November 25, 1955
[4] "Two Boys Lost in Bay", *Suffolk County News*, November 25, 1955

cottages.   The search was continued until dusk Sunday but all that was turned up was a blue jacket, identified as belonging to the Race boy.   It was found in the water at the Cherry Grove dock, two miles west of the scene of the tragedy.   Two shotgun shells were in one of the pockets." [5]

"Scores of volunteers, provided transportation across the bay for eight consecutive days without cost by the Cherry Grove Ferry Service, with Capt. Ken Stein also helping direct searching operations, combed the beach on foot for five miles in both directions in the search for Peter's body.   Daily, cabin cruisers, clam boats, outboard motorboats, the Islip Town police boat and rowboats searched the entire area, equipped with drags and grappling irons. The section was thoroughly searched by Air Force and Coast Guard helicopters and private planes, including several sent aloft by the Civil Air Patrol. [6]

On Monday *"at 11 o'clock searchers reported finding the sunken punt a short distance from the grounded cruiser but the Sprague boy's body was not nearby and the search continued for him with grappling irons.   The small craft was anchored fast and was upright but submerged … in some five feet of water a half mile northeast of the grounded cruiser."* [7]

"Shortly before one o'clock Tuesday afternoon the grappling hooks brought up the two guns and a boot three-quarters of a mile offshore.   Both guns were fully loaded, ruling out the possibility that one of the boys may have been accidently shot." [8]

The search continued through the week.   The searchers scoured every inch of the bay and the Fire Island shore for eight days   …   none hoping to find Pete alive, but wanting to bring his body home, for his family's sake.

Finally on Sunday, November 27[th,]   eight days after the tragedy, Pete's *"body was located by grappling hooks in five feet of water near a point off Fire Island Pines where he and his companion were believed to have tumbled overboard from a capsized skiff.   The discovery of the body … ended one of the most concentrated volunteer searches if its kind ever carried out here.   Young Sprague was located by Charles Norman who was working*

---

[5] "Two Boys Lost in Bay", *Suffolk County News,* November 25, 1955

[6] "Sprague Boy's Body is Recovered", *Suffolk County News,* December 2, 1955

[7] "Two Boys Lost in Bay", *Suffolk County News,* November 25, 1955

[8] Ibid

grappling irons with Emil Novotny aboard Novotny's boat. ...   The spot where the body was found on Sunday was one that had been dragged time and again." [9]

The historical record sheds little light on what actually happened to Larry and Pete on that day.   A speculated scenario is offered in the December 2, 1955, issue of the Suffolk Count News, two weeks after the accident and one week after Pete's body was recovered:

"It is believed that both boys went overboard from an eight foot punt and that young Sprague, who was not a good swimmer, sank while thrashing about in the icy water.   Both were wearing heavy clothing and boots.   Veteran baymen ... familiar with similar accidents in the past, are of the opinion that Race attempted to save his companion after pulling off his heavy jacket and boots, but could not do so, and swam to the cruiser nearby and started for the shore to get help.   He evidently ran the boat aground, jumped overboard to wade ashore but was overcome by exhaustion and cold when within a few feet of the beach.   An autopsy disclosed that his lungs contained sufficient water to list his death as probable drowning." [10]

It was a very trying ordeal, certainly for the Spragues and the Races, but also for the searchers and the entire community as well. Emotionally drained, pained by the tragic loss, each of the searchers must have been shaken by the thought that it could have been his son, and grateful that it wasn't.   Ed Kinkaide was among the Brennan search party that was first on the scene.   Keeping one of the found duck decoys as a symbol of the ordeal, he painted a single word on it ... "Think!" ...   and presented it to his own teenage son. The red-eyed father didn't say a word but the message was clear ... "Life is precious and fragile and the world can be a dangerous place. I love you."

---

[9] "Sprague Boy's Body is Recovered", *Suffolk County News,* December 2, 1955
[10] Ibid

Young Race, an only child, was born on June 25th, 1940, in Mineola, and moved here with his parents in 1953. He was a sophomore at Sayville High School and played on the junior varsity football team. He is survived by his parents, Cecil R. and Agnes Coffey Race. A rosary service was held Tuesday evening at Raynor's Memorial Chapel and a requiem mass held at St. Lawrence's R. C. Church Wednesday morning. Internment followed in St. Lawrence's Cemetery.

--- Suffolk County News, November 25, 1955

Laurance Race

Peter Sprague

Funeral services were held for Peter on Wednesday morning at St. Ann's Episcopal Church, with the Rev. Joseph H. Bond officiating. Internment followed in St. Ann's Cemetery.
Born in Holbrook on September 14th, 1940, Raymond Peter Sprague was a sophomore in Sayville High School where he was active in athletics.
Besides his parents, Radford J. and Lee Ann Dioquardo Sprague, he is survived by a brother, Radford J., Jr., and a sister, Linda.

--- Suffolk County News, December 2, 1955

A final note …

I've always had the greatest respect for the Coast Guard, having seen many of their truly heroic rescues of people in trouble at sea. Conceding that in this case it was too late to even have a chance to save the boys, the performance of the Coast Guard was nonetheless disappointing, at least on the first day.

From an article in the Suffolk County News, April 20, 1956:

"Washington --- Steps have been taken to 'tighten and make more effective' the rescue work of all Coast Guard lifeboat stations as the result of an official inquiry into the deaths of two 15-year old Sayville boys in Great South Bay last November. At the same time a three-man Board of Investigation which convened at Sayville on January 17th and conducted a five-day hearing advised the Commandant here that 'responsibility for this tragedy cannot be attributed to any negligence or incompetence on the part of Coast Guard personnel or to Coast Guard operations in the Sayville area.'

'Under no circumstances,' the board concluded, 'does the evidence indicate that the Coast Guard was responsible for or could have prevented this unfortunate marine tragedy.' "

That is not to say that they were <u>not</u> negligent or incompetent, indeed they were obviously both, just that the tragedy could not be attributed to their negligence or incompetence because both boys were dead before the Coast Guard became involved.

The January 17th hearing is documented in the Suffolk County News of January 20th and 27th, 1956. The detailed testimony reveals a dismal performance by the Coast Guard from the moment they were called, a performance that surely embarrassed a proud organization. If the exposure of their weaknesses led to improvements that may have since saved some lives, then perhaps some good after all will have come from the loss of two fine young men.